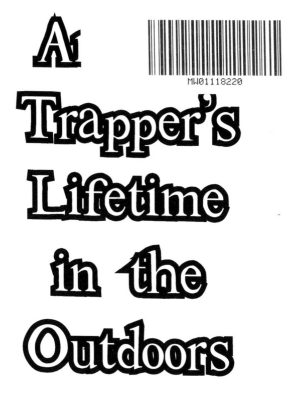

A Trapper's Lifetime in the Outdoors

An autobiography by Larry "Slim" Pedersen

Edited and Published by Kyle Kaatz
Distributed By Kaatz Bros Lures
www.kaatzbros.com
ISBN 978-1-4507-1697-0

Foreword

A s most individuals, I have the need or desire to aspire to attain the level of others greater than myself. Usually in some subject that is close to our hearts, or in an area that greatly peaks our interest. Throughout our lives, we see or come in contact with someone, or maybe if we are lucky a few individuals, we can say that touched us in one way or another. Some of these meetings turn out being good and positive, somewhat memorable, or a mere swing-and-a-miss. As with most of my travels in life, I've been very fortunate to meet people with a much higher cognitive level of understanding. Some of these people leave memories that touch deep within my soul, while others have left without even having scratched the surface.

I had the opportunity to meet Chuck Adams, an avid and renowned big-game bowhunter, several years ago at an outdoors symposium. I had always been in awe of the man, his exploits, and his ability to routinely take trophy game. A quiet person, well known in his industry, someone most in the hunting fraternity would aspire to be like. This man left an impression on me that would later contribute to my ability to seek out others of the same stature and personality. My point being: most people would like to know you as much as you want to know them, but can't unless you make the first step. Some people seem to have a way of answering our questions with a question, which will eventually inspire the answer we seek. Usually it's nothing more than a few thoughtful words, but words that seem to haunt us until finally, with a gasp, we realize and understand the simplistic answer.

Back in 2000 or 2001, early in my haphazard trapping history, I first met another like-minded individual. I aspired to learn at least as much as this man had shrugged off or probably forgotten about wildlife behavior. The man had a certain ease about trapping, as if it were as natural as breathing. His books, studies, and demos were all done with the same laid-back air.

At the 1st Annual Western National Trappers Association convention, in Idaho, I had setup a booth to sell squeaker units. These small animal callers are designed to make chirps and squeaks of birds or rodents to attract predators to trap sets. I had developed my own models after having my last one stolen a few seasons before and wasn't able to find anymore. This process took me a few years to complete and I quickly found that they were a good product to put out to the trapping industry.

Now some of you may wonder what this has to do with the namesake of this book you're now about to study. This gentleman was very instrumental in the original development of the very first squeaker units, which were introduced by Ed Courtney many years ago. Slim Pedersen was Ed's main go-to tester of the units, and without a lot of his studies and time involved with the prototype units, Ed probably would have given up the thought about trying to produce the units altogether. So, I was understandably excited to see that Slim would be at this convention and also be doing a demo. Unknown to me was the fact that he had already been using it in the field, and was impressed with the unit, which was the apogee of success from the man who actually was so instrumental in developing the previous versions. I had studied and watched Slim's tutorials for years. Out here in the West, he's a very well liked and followed trapper and teacher of the arts of trapping and predator studies. Now knowing all of this and seeing he would be here at the convention, I was as giddy as a kid turning his first teenage birthday. I continued to watch and look for him as if I was watching for a parade at a street corner.

As if reading my mind, the indelible Slim sauntered on by, as he passed over my display with others all around trying to hit me with questions about the squeakers. Figuring I had missed my opportunity to introduce myself, I felt nauseous and just wanted to shove everyone away. Here was one of my longtime mentors, whom I had studied and read, watched and tried to learn as much as possible from, walking on by with me not even being able to muster a feeble incoherent "Hello". Again, unknown to me Slim had already done his homework and knew my product and was just waiting until I was not busy to do his own greeting. This never came about until the next day, when I finally mustered up enough courage to walk across the aisle and ask to shake his hand and introduced myself. When he just said, "I know who you are and I have used your product and I'm also impressed with the unit you have created." Dizziness overwhelmed me. My mentor had complimented me and I was losing my footing and I know my coloring was that of a schoolgirl who was caught off guard and embarrassed. None of this was evident in the smile Slim had given me that few minutes I had of his time. I stumbled back over to my booth not even hearing the customers the rest of the day. I had met the one man to me in trapping that had created most of my learning desires and had taught me that being simple and thought-provoking in your attempts at trapping would create many more opportunities than losses.

Since that one or two minutes of his time, Slim has become one of my greatest friends. We have since shared many conventions and times together talking about trapping, friends, and projects. He has also shown to me how much of a practical joker he is, buried so deeply under that almost, quiet demeanor.

One convention we were sharing some time together, I had looked forward to meeting up with him and doing our customary quiet, intellectual studies about nothing in general. This particular night, a group of our friends had planned on all of us going out to a restaurant. As we were seated at a large table, most of us started conversing about life and catching up with each other. I couldn't help but notice Slim digging around in a sack at the end of the table, then he hollered to me to come down there for a bit. Usually, I'm not one for getting up from a table where food will be present soon, and not knowing Slim that well at the time, I obliged. Much to my surprise, he promptly produced a giant red matador's cape, threw it around me and said something about me being the 'bull-stirrer' and finally needing to put the bull down! Well, the cape was okay, as I figured I can go along with a joke or two just as well as anyone, but Slim was not finished there. He dug back in the sack after having ceremonially robed me, and pulled out a matador hat. Where on Earth he found one, I have no idea, and by now I was the attention of half the restaurant, plus those at our table raising such a ruckus of laughter it would've been difficult to hear a fire engine siren! I thought he was finished and tried to step away, when Slim asked where I thought I was going and that he wasn't finished just yet. What could he possibly do to create any more of a scene? Out of his sack, which I then realized had no bottom to it, he pulled a brown bull hat, placed it upon his head and snorted a time or two. I was in sheer shock. Terror had gripped my nether regions and I felt I was going to do things that only little babies did. Then with one last grasp in this bag, he handed me a sword to stab the mighty bull, and proceeded to run around the table snorting like an enraged bull. I honestly thought that the man was either deranged, mad, or on some sort of over-prescribed chemicals. At this time the restaurant was total chaos. Our table could not contain themselves and I figured at any moment the local sheriff was going to show up and arrest the both of us for total annoyance of an establishment. "Stab the mighty bull," was now the cry now from the table, clapping could be heard from the other patrons, so what could I do but stab the mighty beast and hope with all my heart that this would end, which of course it did with yet another masterful theatrical performance from Slim. Woe upon those who under-estimate the wily Slim Pedersen and his masterful art of trickery and mischievousness, for when he makes light of a situation or causes a scene of unending proportions, he is truly masterful.

What more can I say about a person who is quiet, unassuming, humble and more than a testimonial to the trapping heritage we all share and love? I guess that would be the more you think you know and understand a person, the more you really need to learn about them.

I continue to this day to have fond memories of these conventions I shared with Slim and my friends. Of Slim and our projects we worked through, some are on standby, others are producing and I have gained an immense amount of knowledge by being able to have shared a few brief moments of Slims life, and I cannot thank him enough for those moments and more should they arrive.

If you ever have the chance to say "hello" to Slim, don't ever do it with a red robe on!!

- Tom Whiting, Wasatch Wildlife Products

Table of Contents

Introduction

W hen I decided to write about a few of the many thousands of experiences that I have had in the outdoors, I realized that I would be severely criticized by many who view trapping and hunting as cruel and unnecessary in today's world. I thought about what I would need to write to justify myself. I refuse to do so!

I have lived closely with wildlife from the tiny insects to the majestic grizzly bear. This is my world. Spending time in very close contact with nature and even weather extremes has given me a varied knowledge and respect for the great outdoors. It is not an impulsive dream for a perfect world; no pain or misery, where all things get along, through some sort of unrealistic interaction. I contend simply that living in daily, close contact, rather than forming a theory, about how things should or could be perfect, produces awe, wonderment, and love. This goes way beyond anything that the human imagination could ever dream to hope for or put into meaning. Where reality proves that death of one form of life, gives life to another.

The human soul craves contact with nature! I have been one of the very fortunate people who have been able to satisfy this craving. Almost daily contact with nature has made me realize I need to share some of my experiences in the outdoors with people that are not so fortunate. In sharing, my experiences, some may view certain ones as cruel and unnecessary, a thirst for blood. When in reality, many animals face overpopulation in the areas in which they live. The over balance in population of one species leads to stress on others, which normally produces weak unhealthy plants and animals. The animals will probably die a slow and painful death from disease, which is certainly not kind or painless. We must all join together to ensure the future of wildlife through responsible and correct wildlife management. Hunting and trapping are game management agencies tools that we use to responsibly manage wildlife.

I have no idea how many countless times that I have been stuck in the mud or a hard snow drift and after hours of work ended up walking several miles to get help. It would take a whole book to describe most of those experiences, but two that come to mind as being the worst was when returning to my stuck pickup, we found that it had sank deeper into the water, and slimy mud had almost filled the box of the pickup bed. The four wheel drive pickup would not budge it from the muddy draw. We had to go get a tractor to pull it from the mud. Even though that location is fine clay soil, I imagine the ruts we made are still visible today, almost 40 years later.

The other time was after I had walked more than thirty miles to get some help from where I was stuck in mud, only to return way after dark with help, when things had refrozen, and I just drove the pickup away on top of the frozen mud without having to be towed. I have spent many long cold nights with no preparation to spend a night in the outdoors. It just never crossed my mind when I left home that I would spend the night. Maybe one of longest, colder than most, but certainly the most uncomfortable night was spent in a culvert of an old abandoned roadway. I had gotten caught in a heavy snow storm with dropping temperatures, hard winds, and a total whiteout that turned dark when the sun went down. The culvert was the only protection that could be found. One end of the culvert was drifted full of snow, with the opposite end barely visible that I managed to dig open to crawl into to get relief from the hard super cold winds.

Another very cold night was spent huddled under some trees; covered up with the layer of thick pine needles that were under those trees. Fog moved in first, and then it started a misting rain, that soon turned into a steady drizzling rain. Pine needles offer some warmth normally, but they do not stop rain. Once I became wet, I was shivering so hard through the night, that I got up, exhausted and tired the next day, with stiff aching muscles. It was a long, cold, stumbling hike to get back to town.

Caught in a hard cold rain storm, that started to turn into sleet, and eventually snow, I located an old log cabin that was falling in on one end. It got dark fast, but continued to snow. I scraped out an area to lie down, and managed to get a small fire burning.

I curled up and pulled my parka down to partially cover my legs, and managed to fall asleep. Then the wind came up, blowing hard, whipping snow around inside the enclosure, and covered the small fire with snow. I have no idea about how long I actually slept, but it sure didn't seem like as long as I shivered waiting for daylight to arrive. Especially, when the local mouse population found me, because there was several scrambling around on top of me often, and even a couple that attempted to nibble on my hair. I guarantee you that a mouse pulling on one strand of your hair will awaken you from the soundest sleep.

Typical snow drifts in Montana after hard snow storm and high winds.

Anyone who has spent much time setting #330's has a story or two about catching themselves, and I am no exception. The worst situation I found myself in was when I had foolishly fastened a trap to a large exposed tree root on the inside corner of a creek where beavers had the flat lands flooded. The trap was covered with leaves that had floated down the stream. I thought I could remove some of the debris without springing the trap. Famous last words! When the trap went off, it caught me across the bottom of four fingers on my left hand. It rained hard and the water had risen considerably from when I set the trap. I could not get up the steep slick bank to get out of the water, and I could not get to where the trap was fastened. The creek was too deep and running too hard to wade through, and the trap was fastened to a large tree root that was under water deeper than I could reach. I had one hand caught, across the four fingers, and luckily after what seemed like countless attempts, and other founders in the mud that made me slide into the cold water, I did somehow manage to get both jaws fastened down and get out of the trap, but my fingers were blue by that time. It may just be my imagination, but today when that hand gets real cold, I swear those fingers still turn a sickly colored purple.

Working year around, over a vast amount of uninhabited wild country, I have run into many poisonous snakes. I have killed different kinds of poisonous snakes; mostly rattlesnakes—western and eastern as well as timber rattlers, a few copperheads, and more cotton mouth than I care to remember. Although I presently live where coral snakes are reported to live, I have yet to see one.

Since I had worked in loud noise situations, a great deal of the time in my younger years, my hearing has suffered. I can no longer hear rattlesnakes rattle.

I walked down a long, narrow, rocky, ridge to a position that I could observe some coyote pups on the far side of a narrow canyon, hoping to be able to get a shot at one of the adults when they returned home. I thought as I walked down the broken rock ridge that it was a quite likely place to stumble into a rattlesnake, but as I neared the end of the hill, my concentration had centered on the coyote pups, which were playing near the den. I walked to a tall pine tree, and stopped there, leaning against it to break my outline. I had been standing there for at least ten or fifteen minutes, when I shifted my right leg a bit closer to my left leg. As I did, I felt something brushing against that leg. Looking down, I saw that it was the tail end of a rattlesnake, squirming and twisting, rattling like the devil, because I was standing on it with my left foot. The snake was biting my steel toed boot, and venom was running down the front of the boot. When I looked at the snake, I could hear it rattling, but before that, I heard nothing. I decided right then and there, that it was time to break down and go buy a pair of hearing aids.

I have stepped on four rattlesnakes in my lifetime that I am aware of. The first one would have been comical had someone been there to observe it, but at the time it was mostly just scary. I knew what it was the minute I stepped on it, as it buzzed and I felt it squirm under my boot. I jumped, but not like I should have, as I just jumped straight in the air. Cartoon characters, such as Wily coyote, falling and grabbing the air desperately trying to get a hold on anything in order to keep from coming back down, would be a quite accurate description of the way I must have looked. Basketball players hang time would have been envious of my performance, but I finally managed to gather my wits enough to attempt to land on the snakes head when I did come down. The next set of tracks was a long distance from there. All the rest of the snakes I stepped on I always jumped, but never again straight up.

I imagine that any of the snakes could have bitten me, but I honestly suspect that they were as startled as I was and were desperately attempting to get away, rather than bite. Either that or laughing at the fancy new dance moves I was making, putting the younger generation plumb to shame.

Here in Georgia, some of the snakes are huge, as were a few in parts of Texas. However, rattlesnakes all act very similar, and if given a chance, they prefer to get away, rather than attack. A few copper head snakes showed more aggressive temperament, when alarmed, but not anything like many of the cotton mouth snakes exhibit.

I will admit that the cotton mouth snakes scare me more than any of the other kinds do. I always thought they were mostly near water, and guess that most are, but I have killed them in the middle of corn and cotton fields, as well as in tall timber regions, a good distance away from the nearest water. I never know quite what to expect from them, as I have had them come with that white mouth wide open, from at least twenty feet away, making no doubt of their intentions, and I have also had a few attempt to quickly escape, and a few others just lay there looking at me.

The unpredictable cotton mouth snake.

Knowing full well that cotton mouth snakes love to lay around on beaver dams, I had to approach a beaver dam by wading in a small stream, from the lower side of the dam, because of the thick briar brush and vines that bordered the beaver dam. I was very careful as I approached the dam, and even more wary as I climbed on top of it to set a trap on a slide where the beaver were crossing over the dam. Then I went to the bottom side of the dam, and was setting another trap, part way up the slide. After setting the trap, I turned to my right, slightly, looking for a loose limb to place over the trap as a guide. As I started to reach for what appeared to be a perfect two inch around limb, I suddenly realized it was a cotton mouth snake, just laying there watching me. Where it came from, or how it got there without me noticing it is beyond me, but it was quiet, and not moving, just laying there about two feet away from where I was standing in water almost to the top of my hip boots. Not wanting to wade into the snake from my awkward position, with a trapping hammer or one of the light limbs that the dam was constructed from, I just slowly backed away, down the creek. After

I got about five feet away, the snake quickly slid off the dam, into the water where I was. It did not take me very long to quickly slosh through the water, down the creek, to where I could get back out of the creek, where the brush and vines were not so thick.

Scrambling down the creek, I stirred up a good deal of muddy water, which the current carried to the opposite bank from where I quickly got out of the creek. Evidently the snake had followed my mud streak, because it crawled out of the water on the opposite side of the creek from where I had climbed out. My pickup was parked a few feet away, and getting my .22 rifle, I returned to the creek and shot the snake on the opposite bank.

Another time, I was pulling a beaver out of the water, from where it had slid down the drowning wire, and a cotton mouth snake appeared from nowhere, following the beaver up onto the bank, as I pulled the dead beaver up onto dry ground. As I said, I never know where to expect one, or where one will show up. I even had one drop from some trees, which is a dimension that just never seems to register in my mind, until something draws attention to that area.

When I was very young, someone in my family found a baby deer that was barely able to walk, and had brought it home. While I can barely remember anything at all about it, and sometimes wonder if I actually can remember, or just believe that I can from the many stories I have heard over the years. At any rate, I guess that the fawn, a pup cocker spaniel dog, a large house cat, and I use to play hide and seek games. The deer would seek each of us out, then jump, kick, and run when it located one of the hiders. As I said, I can barely remember any of it.

Deer were not very plentiful, anywhere at that time, even though the population was on the increase. I guess some hunter shot the pet deer on the lawn in front of our house.

I do very vaguely remember a group of men sitting around the living room discussing deer hunting, and like always, the talk was about this big buck and that one. I also faintly remember seeing two small dead deer lying in the back of an old pickup truck. I remember that incident, because I was surprised that the animals had been cut open, and all the entrails were removed, and I vaguely remember asking about that.

After my grandmother and I had moved into town, I remember the neighbors having deer hung up in their garage to age, before they were skinned and cut up to eat. So I suppose that deer hunting, or perhaps, just hunting in general was something that I was exposed to at a very early age, as I also remember seeing dead pheasants and Hungarian grouse before they were skinned and prepared for eating. Funny as it may seem, I remember the smell of the dead pheasants and grouse, as well as anything else about them, and of course the men talking about shooting them with shotguns, and what a great shot this was or that guy made.

Not having a father around, I would long for the times when my uncle would come around, and it was usually when he was hunting or fishing that he would stop to visit my grandmother and me. So I suppose I wanted to become a good hunter to gain some respect, or to attempt to be like my uncle.

After my grandmother made the mistake of showing me where the .410 shotgun was located, as well as the shells, so I could go shoot the skunk in the trap inside the chicken house, I managed to sneak it out of the house to go hunting. I knew where some pheasants lived, so I snuck up close and shot one, on the ground, since I had no idea they could be shot while flying. When I got home, I snuck the gun back into the house, then went outside and brought in the pheasant. My grandmother was pleased to have the pheasant for food. I told her I had shot it with my bow and arrow.

Then one day I had snuck the gun from the house, and was again attempting to sneak up on some pheasants that were running ahead of me in some thick willow brush. The clump of willows, growing along the edge of a small dry creek, ended where an old road crossed the dry stream bed. When I came quickly around the willows to the open area, a small spike buck whitetail deer came around the same clump of willows from the opposite side of the stream. Unaware by either of us that the other was around, we suddenly met in the open area.

I have replayed the incident over in my mind many times, and still wonder why I cocked the gun, and raised it. I do remember aiming for the white spot on the neck, just under the chin, and thinking that if I was a real deer hunter, I would shoot it right there. Then something made me pull the trigger! The deer just dropped like a bag of rocks.

Happy and excited one minute, then scared and worried the next, because I knew that deer season wasn't open, I quickly ran to inspect the dead deer, then I ran to both sides of the willows to be certain that no one had heard the shot, and was coming to investigate. Then, still scared and concerned, I sat down on top of the deer to figure out what I was going to do.

I had heard people cuss a deer poacher that would just shoot a deer and leave it lay to rot, and waste the meat, so I figured I needed to gut it out. In my pocket I had a very dull old pocket knife that I used to cut sticks and carve on wood. Even though I had seen deer with their entrails removed, I had no clue exactly how to go about doing it. So after a lot of struggling, I managed to get the deer lying on its back, then while sitting straddling over the carcass, I took the knife and stabbed it into the stomach where I figured I needed to open the carcass. The ensuing gasses that came blowing from the opening were nauseating, but with the knife still deeply embedded I attempted to slit open the length of the carcass, while green goo and glop, started to spill out of the opening. With the dull little knife, I was unable to open the rib cage, so just started pulling out some entrails, cut that off, then pull out some more to cut off again. The stomach contents had spilled when I first jabbed in the knife, and it was not an easy chore, as more would come out each time I cut off a piece of the intestines.

After I had removed everything that I thought I could, I picked up the shotgun and walked home. When I walked into the house, my grandmother let out a blood curdling scream. Yelling, she said, "I told you never to play with that gun, where did you shoot yourself?"

After I got her to settle down, and explained to her what I had done, my grandmother was happy one minute then angry again the next, so she went from scolding me to praising me.

After some time of debating what we should do, she took out a pen and paper, roughly drew a deer carcass, and showed me where to cut to quarter it. Then she took out her favorite "Old Town" butcher knife, gave it a couple of quick strokes on the back side of another old butcher knife to quickly hone the edge, and shoved the handle towards me. All the while scolding me to not dare break or lose that knife.

So back into the woods I went. Again, I had seen deer after they were skinned, but had no clue how to go about skinning one, and all my grandmother had told me to do was skin it, then cut it where she had drawn on the paper, so I could drag home a quarter of the deer, one at a time.

So using the large old knife, I would skin off a basketball size chunk of skin, cut it off, throw it away, and then repeat the process again. By the time I had it skinned, I had deer hair on everything. I roughly got it quartered up, and managed to drag it home one quarter at a time. The meat was covered with entrails contents, dirt, sticks, and leaves when I took it into the house. It probably should have been almost inedible, but as I remember it was delicious!

Against my grandmother's wishes, I managed to eventually save enough money to buy a used single shot JC Higgins .22 rifle. I used that gun to shoot a lot of wild cottontail rabbits, and then shot a doe mule deer in the side of the head. I was older and had seen a deer cleaned by that time, and had much less trouble with that second deer. I just recently gave that old rifle to my youngest son to give to my two grandsons. All of my own children learned to shoot with that old rifle.

Then some time later, I talked the local hardware store manager into letting me put money down on a used .270 Remington rifle. It took me almost six months to pay for the rifle, and a box of shells, so that when I was twelve years old I could legally hunt for deer. My uncle was supposed to take me hunting, but he never showed up the first day of season. So the next weekend I took the gun and walked several miles out of town. I shot a small two point mule deer, cleaned it, walked back home, then talked the neighbor man into going with me in his old pickup truck to haul it home.

Since I never had any money, it was natural that I would become good friends with a classmate at school that had thirteen brothers and sisters, and an alcoholic father. That family and I survived on poached deer meat, so we had that much in common. The fact that we were friends, and that I was his only friend, resulted in the two of us hunting deer together often for the next few years. His mother trapped muskrats in the stream that ran beside their home, and I learned a bit about trapping muskrats while spending time at their home.

A friend and I about to drag out a spike bull elk.

The Mule deer population at that time was exploding. I became an avid deer and elk hunter for several years. I spent many days and nights hunting deer and elk in the high mountains.

Since I was never prepared to spend a night, there were some very cold nights that I could tell about, while huddled in pine needles without a fire. There are a few hunting incidents that stand out in my memory, that I could tell about, but will just relate a couple stories here: one is about the largest deer that I ever shot, and another is a bit longer story about the largest deer that I ever saw, but did not shoot.

When a hard snow storm would settle in on the high mountains, the mule deer and elk would begin to migrate down the mountains to lower elevations where the snow would not get so deep. I remember sitting in one place with field glasses, counting over three hundred deer, in groups of from two to twenty, as they slowly came down off the high slopes. I saw some large bucks in those groups, but because of the deep snow, there was no way to even walk close enough to get a shot at most of them. So I picked out the largest deer that seemed to be close enough. I would have to struggle through the deep snow to get close enough to shoot.

The area is located where the high tall mountains meets a lower area of high, more rolling, foothills type of landscape with timbered ridges on the north slope and open areas on the southern slopes. I was skirting around the bottom of a very tall steep mountain, attempting to intercept five deer winding through the timber and open areas, as they migrated away from the higher mountains on the other side of the stream. I had seen a large buck with them, rutting hard, nosing the does he was pushing ahead of him. The snow was deep even at that elevation, and the going was very slow and difficult. I found myself stopping often to catch my breath in the cold air. Each time I would stop, I would attempt to glass ahead through the binoculars, in order to keep track of the deer that were moving quicker than I was, as they descended from the mountains on the other side of the stream that I was following.

Although I was attempting to watch the deer ahead and to my right, a smaller but very steep mountain was to my left, and when I stopped, I caught motion high above me on the mountain. Using my field glasses to look at the area, I saw a black bear wading through some deep snow. It was only about six or seven hundred yards above me. I had never shot a bear before, and it suddenly took on more interest than the deer did. Even though it was high above on a very steep slope, I decided to try for the bear instead of the deer I had been watching.

Climbing that steep slope however proved to be next to impossible in the snow that was close to three feet deep. My feet would slip on the slick snow covered granite rocks, and the rocks themselves would want to give way and roll downward under my feet, as I struggled to gain some elevation to the same level I had spotted the black bear. I would often have to strain, to grab a hold on some small brush to keep some balance and keep from sliding back down the steep slope.

My plan was to get to where I had seen the black bear then follow the tracks in the snow to where I could get a shot. Seemed like a good plan, but the steepness of the slope and the deep snow, soon played me out physically, even though I was in very good physical shape at the time from playing football all fall and basketball in the early winter. As I slowly gained some elevation, the steepness of the slope seemed to give way a little bit, and I finally managed to locate the bear tracks to follow through some ragged lodge pole pine trees.

Following the bear tracks in the soft snow, through the timber, soon proved more difficult than I thought it would be too. Deer tracks were everywhere in the timber, and since the loose snow was deep, it was often difficult to separate the bear tracks from all the deer trails through the low brush, and broken down timber in the wind twisted and tangled trees on that steep slope.

When I finally managed to follow what I believed was the bear tracks, out of the timber into a small open area, I again spotted some motion, going into the next clump of timber on the opposite side of the opening. Raising my gun to use the scope, I saw that there were three deer standing there looking at me. One of them was a very large buck.

I suddenly found myself having to make a decision. I needed to decide if I should shoot that large deer, or continue and hope to get a shot at the bear that I had seen quite a long time before by that time. I really wanted that bear, since I had already shot some very respectable buck deer in years before.

My friends that I hung out with at that time were all avid deer hunters. Because the deer were so thick, it became a thing to see who would get the largest buck each year, but it also became a thing to not kill any mule deer that did not have a thirty inch wide spread between the antlers. Number of points was somewhat of a criterion to judge, but because many deer were killed each year with tangle messes of points going every which direction, and almost all of the larger bucks always seemed to have massive bases and heavy horns, the spread seemed to be the thing that was sought the most for bragging rights.

I remember one friend who shot one of the nicest mule deer racks I have ever seen suffer some bad razzing from all of us because it only had a 28 inch spread. Truth is, we were probably all jealous as that deer had six perfectly matched points on each antler and they were heavy and tall.

Tired, and a bit frustrated with the steepness of the mountain, and the deep snow, I was very tempted to shoot the large buck, but I really wanted that bear instead of just another deer. I gave up on the idea of shooting the deer and started to slowly walk again, along the tracks that I was following. Then the tracks crossed over a fallen log, and it became very obvious that I was not following the bear, but somehow had managed to get off the bear tracks and was actually just following a deer trail. I stopped there, trying to think about where I might have messed up, when the deer on the other side of the clearing began to move again. Two does started to trot, up the hill, and the buck came out of the timber to follow. When he did, my mouth almost dropped, as he was the widest spread deer I had ever seen. I kneeled, and easily shot him from a distance of about one hundred yards. The deer dropped quickly, and then began kicking, and when it did, it started to tumble straight down the mountain. Because of the steepness of the hill, and the slick snow, it rolled and slid almost all the way to the bottom of the mountain.

The deer had six very distinct long points on one antler and seven points on the other antler. The horns were thirty seven inches wide, outside measurement, and I do not know or remember if I ever did actually measure inside measurement. I have long skinny fingers, but I could not put my hand around the base of the horns. I do remember, that it was around ten in the morning when I shot it, and it took the rest of the day, and was well past dark by the time I managed to get the large deer drug to where I could get a vehicle to load it.

Later after the horns had been cut from the skull, and shown to anyone with enough patience to listen to my bragging about them, they were thrown on top of the chicken house with all my other horns that were accumulated over the years. That entire pile of deer horns were stolen, a few years later, when my grandmother died, while I was married and living in a different part of the state. Several years later I saw the large horns again in a taxidermy shop. The taxidermist had just bought the rack from a man who said he did not have enough money to get it mounted. When I told him the story about the horns, he looked them over again, and agreed that the rack was several years old. However I did not get it back, as I did not have the money he asked for it.

I believe that the largest mule deer that I ever saw was the following year, from the time I had shot the large one I just described. Three of my friends and I had hiked, up the bottom of a long creek between mountains on each side. It had been a long hike, and although the snow was only five or six inches deep, it had not been an easy hike, and we were all tired when we spotted the deer ahead of us. The buck was nosing some does around in some tall willow brush, and it was impossible to gauge just how large he really was, but it was quite evident that he was massive. They were a good mile ahead of us, and we all just quickly decided we had fooled around and already walked farther than we wanted to attempt to drag a deer out of that rugged terrain of large granite boulders and fallen down timber unless it was a real monster.

That canyon was noted for producing large deer over the years before, but since I was the only one that knew how to get into the canyon, the friends I was with talked me into taking them into the area so they could attempt to shoot a large buck. I was the only one that was in good physical condition, and the other three had already been whining and wanting to go back when we saw the deer. There was a lot of grumbling about not wanting to shoot a deer that far away from a vehicle all of a sudden. I was a bit disgruntled, but told them I would try to get around the deer and perhaps chase them back towards where they were and then they could decide if they wanted to shoot it. There was some more discussion about me not shooting the darn thing way back there if it did prove to be a super large deer.

Getting to the deer again proved to be more difficult and a bit farther than I had earlier estimated. It took quite a bit of time to get to where the deer were, and I could see that there was no way to easily get behind the deer to haze them to where the others were, so I just decided I would attempt to get close enough to judge how large the buck really was. As I attempted to get close, the deer saw me, and began to trot away. I was only about two hundred yards away at that point, and could easily have shot the big buck, but I had already decided that I would not shoot it no matter how big it was, as struggling through the terrain was difficult enough without attempting to drag a large deer through that tangled mess.

I was very tempted to shoot the buck when I saw that it really was huge, and larger than any other deer that I had ever seen, with a nice even rack, as I studied it though my scope. Afraid that temptation was going to get the better of my good judgment, I loaded a round in the chamber, aimed slightly to one side of the buck, and shot a rock, to scare the deer farther into the canyon.

I know I said that I was only going to tell two deer stories, but if you will bear with me just a bit longer, I feel like I should tell you about a nice whitetail deer that I shot with my bow.

About a mile away from the higher mountains, there is a long hill that is not too high that just sort of sticks up out of more flat rolling terrain. One side of the hill is bare and open grass, while the other side of the steep hill is covered with plum thickets and chokecherry brush. I had seen five mule deer go into the thick scrub brush side of the hill, shortly after full daylight. I drove around to the bare side of the hill where the deer could not see me approaching, parked my vehicle there, and walked to the top of the hill. Not wanting to skyline myself when I crossed over the top, I got down onto my hands and knees and crawled through a low swale of the hill. As I neared the brush, I ran into a barbed wire fence line that I did not know was there, and I stopped there and stood up, pondering how to cross the fence line without making it creak and give my presence away. Standing there, I caught some motion along the same fence line ahead of me.

The bow that I had was a homemade long bow. A handyman neighbor of where I worked in the summer months had made the bow by splitting some dry cotton wood, then used a piece of raw hide on the back to keep it from splitting out when it was used, and he had hand forged a steel handle around it in the middle. It drew at over sixty pounds. It was quite long, and because it was so long,

I could not get a decent string long enough for the bow, so I had used a piece of baler wire. It worked for about ten shots, then would break, and have to be replaced. I talked the man into selling me the bow; as I could not afford a real fiberglass recurve bow. It was long and a bit clumsy, and I was not strong enough to hold it at full draw of a 28 inch cedar arrow, for more than just a very brief time. I had practiced with it and gotten pretty decent shooting it when I could stand, but where I was in that brush, next to that fence line, just drawing that long bow was going to be difficult.

The motion I had seen, I had assumed was from the mule deer that I had saw at daylight, but instead it proved to be a nice whitetail buck walking along the fence line, coming closer to my position. Moving slowly, I struggled to raise the bow, and get into as good a shooting position as would be possible, without moving too quickly to alert the approaching deer. I did not want to attempt a head on shot if at all possible, but the deer looked up and saw me. He did not know what I was and was attempting to figure out what I was. I was afraid to move, so did not attempt to draw the bow. So we remained there for a long time, just staring at each other. The deer stomped one foot and snorted. When it did, there was some motion, breaking some brush below our level, further into the thick scrub brush. He turned and looked towards that noise, which gave me a chance to draw and quickly get away an arrow. The arrow hit the deer in the neck, and he went down instantly.

Feeling very lucky, I hurried to the deer, and could see that it was not dead, so I took out my hunting knife and proceeded to try to cut its throat. However, as I held onto one antler with my left hand, and started to stick the knife in behind the windpipe, the deer suddenly threw its head and stood up, pushing me back into the fence. Then it dropped its head and charged forwards. Releasing my hold on the knife which was still stuck in the side of the buck's throat, I grabbed a hold of the other antler, just as his lunge drove one tine of his horns through my pants and into my leg, just above my right knee. I fell through the rusty old fence line, while maintaining my hold on the antlers. The deer was very strong and struggling to get away, but I managed to get one horn hooked around a strand of the barbed wire and gained a bit of leverage advantage. That gave me a chance to release my hold on that horn, and again get a grip on the knife, which I then used to severe the windpipe and juggler vein.

For a brief time, it had seemed like it was going neck and neck with the hunter bagging the deer or the deer bagging a hunter. The young whitetail deer only had four points on each side, and they were not very heavy, but rather long and slender, making it easy for the deer to push the one point through my pants and into my leg. Luckily, most of the actual damage done was to my pride, as the dull horn just poked a hole, did no serious internal damage, and the wound bled out clean.

There were only a few Pronghorn Antelope on top of the lower hills in the valley where the tops of those hills were flat, before the top of the hill ended at the next drainage that then ran down into a river. A class mate drew an antelope license, and asked if I knew where any were. Everyone knew that I was always walking the hills, and usually knew where most animals were located. When I told him I knew where some always hung out, he asked if I would show him.

Since I did not yet own a car, he picked me up in his father's new car. We were to use the car to get to where we were going to hunt, and then walk from there. When we got close to the area I had planned on hunting, we saw a young buck antelope in a stubble field. Don grabbed his 30-06 rifle and jumped out on his side of the car. I picked up the binoculars and started to watch the antelope. When he shot, my head reverberated from the concussion and loud noise. The antelope just stood there, and I saw dust fly high behind the young buck. I told him he hit high. He shot again, and again dust flew way behind the antelope, but I told him to hold up, and not shoot again until I get out of the car, the loud noise was unbearable.

When I jumped out of the vehicle, I turned to make sure he was not going to shoot again right away. When I did, I saw two long creases in the top of the car. He had rested the gun on the top of the car, aimed through the scope, and when he shot the curve of the new ford car was in front of the barrel. I was very lucky, as one crease had opened a crack, but the bullet went up, and not down through, or it more than likely would have hit me in the head. Needless to say, he did not get to borrow his dad's car for any more hunting trips!

As I am writing this today, I believe I need to tell the readers that I have not shot a deer, elk, or antelope for many years. I love the meat; however, since my family is all grown and left home, friends who do love to hunt usually supply me with what wild game meat I might need.

I suppose that I have come full circle in some ways. Like most who hunt, I felt like I was pitting my skills against the game that I was pursuing, my love for the outdoors kept pushing me, as it does yet today in a much different way. Today, if I feel a need to test my skills, I find the use of a video camera much more difficult than other hunting. Use of a video camera means you must get close in order to get good pictures and that does not just mean sneaking with proper use of the wind, motion, and noise, but also light angles as well. I have miles and miles of HI8 video tape that I am very proud of.

Initially I suppose I started hunting, just wanting to shoot something, like I believe most hunters do today. Then I wanted to get a trophy. For a few years after that I kept telling myself I needed the meat to help raise my growing family. As time quickly passed, I was able to make a living in the outdoors daily; struggling with smart coyotes doing predator control work, and that challenge replaced other desires. I know for a fact that I have probably been one of the more fortunate people in the world, because I have been able to make a decent living, doing the work that I would do if I had spare time to enjoy myself.

For as long as I can remember I have been in awe of many things in nature. I remember spending time studying red and black ants in the mounds that they create to make a home for their colonies. Being young and full of curiosity, I just had to learn what would happen if I took a shovel full of ant hill from a black ant colony and dropped it onto a red ant hill, and of course that was not good enough, then I had to try black to red, and then red ant hill to red ant hill and black to black etc.

I also remember pulling the long jumping legs off of grasshoppers, then throwing them onto the ant hills, as well. The ants

The Black Locust.

would swarm the larger grasshoppers but were mostly not capable of denting the armor shield of the grasshoppers. Perhaps I should have become an entomologist.

Dwelling on this a bit at this time, I just realized that I have not seen a black ant in several years. Hmmm guess I will have to return to Absarokee, Montana now and search for some black ants, as I see red ants of many different sizes everywhere. I even remember ants that had red posteriors and a black anterior, although they were not too plentiful like solid red or solid black ants. Where I live now in Southern Georgia, I see way more little red fire ants than I care to see.

A couple of different times in my life, I started a butterfly collection. Once when I was quite young, perhaps nine or ten years old, and again later while in college, studying biology, I started a complete insect collection. I must admit that yet today, I find insects very interesting, and often waste time just observing them. Temptation is always there to attempt to catch a strange butterfly or moth, or a "rarey" as a friend who was also an avid collector would have referred to them.

I always find it interesting, how animals in different parts of the country will do things differently. By way of a couple quick examples, yellow jacket wasps in the north will build a paper like home inside buildings, or broken trees, while the same, or at least very similar, insect in the south will build nests under the ground. Perhaps it is the snow and hard freezing temperatures in the north that force the difference.

Whitetail deer in the north are very large in comparison to whitetail deer in the south or on both coastlines.

I have never been too well versed on botany, but it is impossible not to notice many similarities as well as differences in where and how plants and trees grow.

Maybe one of the strangest trees that I have ever seen was in Missouri. I have never looked it up to find the name, but it grows clumps of long thick sharp thorns on the trunk of the tree as well as on every branch. No climbing animal of any kind could ever scale up that tree, and anyone driving a vehicle had best not get too close or drive over any broke off branches, as the thorns are long and hard enough to penetrate a tire easily. One area was a quite thick area of those trees, perhaps a hundred acres or more on both sides of a small trickling stream of water. (Note: This tree is the Black Locust.)

Traveling around to different parts of the USA trapping, I often find myself aware of the different smells in different parts of the country. The Desert Southwest always seemed to smell of greasewood, while Montana always smells of sagebrush or pines, as does Wyoming and Idaho, yet Utah seems to have another dominate odor that I have never quite been able to put my finger on. Iowa and Missouri always have corn dust hanging in the air that will cover a vehicle when it rains. Here in the South East, when not near an atomic power plant, the dominate odors are usually of damp pines or a musky wet odor, often of swamps and swamp gas, unless near large civilization areas in summer when flowering plants will dominate the air odors.

Spending the time that I do in the outdoors, I often find myself marveling as I watch some quite simple act of nature. I probably waste much more time than I should just observing things. Again by way of a couple quick examples, I have always found the dung ball beetles a very strange and curious little creature, as they make balls from cow dung, then roll the balls around backwards with their rear legs, seeking the perfect place to dig a hole to put the balls into and lay their eggs.

In the Desert Southwest I found most of the vegetation of interest, as well as several interesting little lizards scampering around, not to mention the roadrunner birds. I also spotted a couple little wild rodents of some sort scampering around in the higher rocky hills of the desert that I have never been able to identify that I would love to learn more about.

In the southeast I find myself very curious about the nature of possums, and armadillos. Yes, I know, but I do find them interesting anyway, as I have never lived anywhere where they were before now. I also find the many different kinds of turtles quite interesting, especially the endangered land living Terrapin turtles, or Gophers as they are referred to here in Georgia, because of all the large holes they make to live in.

Just as another side note about the Terrapin turtles, I would see a quite large one daily lying in front of his hole, he would scramble quickly back down the hole as I drove or walked closer. One day, I was eating crackers as I drove past, and stopped at the hole, put a few cracker in the entrance to see if it would eat them. This started to become a daily thing, and I noticed that the turtle would not go in the hole until I got real close, and it would not go too deep, I started talking to it, just saying dumb things, like here is your morning snack again, and saw that the turtle would emerge to eat before I had walked away very far. I found that interesting. As summer quickly came, I got a cell phone call, and that area has poor cell phone reception, so I stopped my vehicle, and stepped out where I could walk up onto a high place to take the call. Standing there talking on the phone, here came the turtle. He would cock his head and listen, then scramble a few scampering steps towards me. I am sure he was thinking he was going to get some more crackers. Guess it surprised me, to realize that a turtle was that smart.

In the Northwest, where I grew up, I also always marveled at the friendly little Horney toads.

As a sideline note, I also always find it interesting how people everywhere accomplish many of the same things, but use some different means to do so. I find it very interesting how people reach the same conclusion, but use a totally different thought process to reach the conclusions.

I know that I cannot explain it, but while spending time observing things in the outdoors, I always feel some sort of closeness or a contact of some kind anyway, with the things that I observe.

Perhaps my youngest son put it into context better than I could when he said, "Dad, you take the time to look at things that other people only see."

❖ ❖ ❖

Early one morning, in a light foggy mist that made the air smell very clean yet heavily tainted with the odor of cedar because both sides of the narrow ridge I was walking down were overgrown with cedar shrubs; I caught quick motion ahead. I was searching for a coyote den, and thought that perhaps the quick darting motion may have been a coyote. I stopped where I was, attempting to strain to tell if perhaps the almost undetectable light breeze direction may have changed, to alert animals to my presence. I had been moving slowly, and quietly, so I felt certain it had not been noise that gave away my presence. Then staring in the general direction that I had seen the motion, I saw a whitetail deer running hard, followed quickly by a second deer.

My first thoughts were that perhaps a coyote was chasing the deer, but as I watched them, it soon became apparent that the one doe was actually chasing the other one and that she meant business as her ears were laid down, backwards, and she was kicking with her front feet towards the other deer.

Over the years, I have watched both whitetail and mule deer does chase each other for short distances, usually while grazing in a meadow, and I always figured it was a bit of a competition thing for the tender best morsels; however I have never seen them act up with quite the intensity that these two deer were carrying on.

They went out of my sight, over the next low ridge, and I again started walking slowly down the game trail that I had been following, where fresh coyote tracks were leading. I had not gone too far, when I saw one doe coming back over the far ridge, and hurry quickly, obviously with some destination in mind. I lost sight of her in the cedars when she started up the same ridge that I was on.

My mind wandered at that point, returning to the fresh coyote tracks that I had been following down the narrow winding game trail. I continued my slow progress ahead, but again detected motion on the far ridge. It was the other doe sneaking back, very slowly, straining to look ahead. It was obvious she was watching the other deer, as she was staring in the direction I had last seen that deer.

I moved slowly down the trail again, using my hand to reach ahead, and pull a low hanging branch away from the trail. I caught motion ahead and below. It was the first deer that had returned over the far ridge, and she was turning around in tight circles. Thinking that was quite odd, I again stopped to watch, and raised my rifle to look at the deer through the scope.

Watching the deer spinning I detected the front legs and head of a fawn hanging from under her tail. The second deer had stopped her progress to observe from the opposite side of the small draw. I did not get to see the fawn completely emerge, but it became apparent that the birth had completed when the deer stopped spinning and started to pay attention to something I could not see on the ground in the tall grass.

At that time, the other deer again began to come forward and approach the doe that had just given birth. The new mother heard her approaching, and quickly raised her head from the duties she had been paying attention to on the ground, and gave a short quick chase again, with ears laid back, but, she quickly returned to her fawn. The other deer had gone part way up the opposite side of the draw and stopped to stare back at the pair below my position.

The new Mother was paying attention to her baby, but then suddenly twisted around, stopped, and turned her head towards her tail. She arched her back, then started to twist around again, and suddenly another fawn just dropped while she spun.

As the new mother began licking on her second new born baby, the other deer again began to slowly approach the new family. The new mother was going to have no part of it, and she one more time chased the other doe from the immediate area.

Feeling very fortunate to have witnessed what I had, I began attempting to figure a route that I could use to sneak away, hoping not to disturb the deer. As I looked up the ridge, and towards the head of the small draw, I saw some more motion at the very head of the draw. At first, I just figured it was probably another deer, but then it came around a large clump of cedars, and I could see that it was a coyote coming towards the deer.

I did not want to disturb the new family, but it was quite apparent what the coyote had on his mind as he quickly moved through the cedars, intently looking at the deer. I sat down in an open area, used my shooting sticks to brace the rifle and shot him.

One doe ran over the far ridge, and the new mother started to follow, but stopped half way up the other side of the low ridge.

Feeling a bit guilty, yet feeling good too, about what I had just done, I walked higher up the ridge that I was on to make a wide swing away from the birth area, as I went to the dead coyote. I drug the carcass towards the head of the draw, and over the hill to make a very wide swing around the area. I was hoping that I would get to see the new mother return to her new born fawns, but she went over the hill in the direction the first deer had ran instead.

I know how nervous a new mother can be, and that if they become too upset, they may abandon their babies. I hoped that she would return and reclaim her new born when I left the area. I would like to report that she had, but will admit that I never did find out for sure. It was several days before I ever returned to that area again, and while I did check the place I had seen the fawns born, I never found any sign that anything had ever happened there. Not knowing for certain, my conscience still bothers me a bit about it all, but as I reason it out, if the new mother did abandon her babies, the results would have been the same if I had not shot the coyote, as it was obvious what he would have done had he been allowed to get to the new family.

❖　❖　❖

Birds have been another fascination of mine. When I was about ten, I brought home a young magpie and raised it in a rabbit hut cage that I stood upright so the bird could hop onto sticks that I placed across the pen. That magpie would squawk all the time, sometimes excitedly, as it would jump and flit from stick to stick.

The neighbor lady that lived in a house just across the board fence line that the cage stood next to had several children and a little dog that she called Tipi. Just a brief description of the woman: Quite large, only saw her with shoes on one time, and only wore a tent like loose skirt all the time. She would call her Tipi dog about ten times a day, by standing on her front porch yelling rapidly at the top of her lungs, "Here tipi, here tipi, here tipi, here tipi."

One day when I was going into my home, the lady stormed across the yard, grabbed me by my arm and shook the heck out of me, yelling, "If you don't knock it off, I am going wail your pants, good!"

When I said, "I haven't done anything," she stormed off saying, "If I catch you I am going to use my belt to beat you!"

My grandmother heard and saw the whole performance and asked me what I had been doing, and did not believe me when I said nothing.

Two days later she again came to the house, only to apologize that time. It seemed the magpie had learned to talk listening to her call the dog, and whenever she would call it, the magpie would begin imitating her. She had thought it was me making fun of her. The old gal was a tough callous old gal, and was always cussing her children, husband, or dog, and it wasn't too long before the magpie was cussing like a sailor as well.

My grandmother became upset with the bird one day, since she did not like it in the first place, she had became tired of all the cussing, and so she hobbled outside with her crutches, and released it. Bad mistake actually, as the bird would not leave, and lived in the neighborhood, flying around eating from garbage cans or pet food on people's porch. It would sit in trees cussing up a blue streak. It had all the little old ladies that lived in that area very upset. I have no idea what ever became of the bird, as one day it just disappeared, but I suspect someone finally got tired of its cussing; enough to take matters into their own hands.

Perhaps I need to tell another story about the large neighbor lady. She wanted a baby skunk for a pet, and knowing that I was always catching them, she told me she would give me five dollars for a live baby skunk.

I made a rough box trap, from a produce crate, with the door just large enough for a skunk to enter into, but I did not put a bottom on the cage. When I caught a baby skunk in the box trap, I went next door and told the old gal about it, but told her I did not know how to get it out of the box trap. She went with me, all excited and happy to get her new pet.

She got down on her hands and knees to lift up the crate, and reach for the skunk. Now I want the readers to get an image of this. Her dress rose up over her huge hips, and bunched up under her arms. She had on nothing under the dress, and I was standing directly behind her, not wanting to get sprayed. Despite all that was exposed, my memory is mostly about the road map of all the large varicose veins.

When she managed to get a hold of the skunk's tail, grinning her almost toothless smile, she proudly held it up and turned around to show me. There was a large glob of yellow ooze slowly sliding down her forehead, and a very strong familiar odor filled the air.

I could elaborate a bit on the story about that little skunk, as I helped the would-be taxidermist who had convinced her that he could de-scent the animal. After using ether from a spray can used to start diesel trucks in cold weather to partially put the skunk to sleep, he simply cut off the nipples protruding from the rear of the skunk, and sewed them up. It kind of worked, as the skunk would only smell a little when it got very excited after that time. It did eventually make an interesting pet, and what I remember best is how much fun it was to watch it catch grasshoppers by pouncing upon them with its front feet, then quickly gulp them down. Learning how near sighted it was also proved interesting as well as valuable information for the years to follow.

Going back to magpies for a few more lines; over time, I have learned to watch magpies and crows closely. The sharp eyed rascals from their elevated positions will see animals long before I do. If they see a predator they will fly to it. If they see deer or elk, they will fly towards them, and then land in the trees nearby. While hunting, I always keep a sharp eye on the birds to see where they go, how, and why, as it will often alert me to other animals that I would never have seen otherwise; especially while calling wildlife with calls.

When I was young, I was always bringing home some wild animal to keep as a pet. My grandmother was not too fond of many of the things I brought home, and just like the magpie, I suspect she released many of them. However she fell in love with a little chipmunk that I brought home, and the chipmunk eventually had the run of the house, but would return to it's cage were it had a nice coffee can full of cotton for a bed.

Another pet that I brought home that my grandmother fell in love with was a rock chuck. An animal similar to a wood chuck, only the rock chucks live in rockslides. It was very small when I brought it home, and we needed to borrow a doll baby bottle to feed it at first. My grandmother was upset at me for taking it away from its mother, so her maternal instincts took over. It wasn't long, and her daily routine was to have it sitting in her lap on the rocking chair, like a cat would do. The dog, cat, and rock chuck often slept together. As it grew we put it out on the lawn where it would feed on the clover, but we had to build a fence and a small house for it to hide in, as the neighborhood dogs did not like it at all.

One day in the fall it just disappeared. After a lot of searching, we decided that perhaps one of the dogs had finally gotten it.

I lived in the basement of the one room home, and my grandmother had difficulty getting up and down the stairs. One day in the winter she started complaining that I had something stinking up the house in the basement. There was no peace to be had, until I helped her get down the stairs and we searched every nook and cranny that we could get into, as my grandmother was also a bit of a packrat and had boxes and boxes of stuff stored there. Two days later, she asked me to help her move the rollaway couch bed that she slept on at night, and was a couch in the daytime. In the back corner of that couch, the rock chuck had chewed a hole through the bottom lining, curled up there, and was hibernating. The droppings and urine were causing the stink in the house. We fixed him up a box. In the spring, I took him a far distance out of town and released him in a sandstone rockslide.

A couple years later, I brought home a very small porcupine. While it would seem unlikely, the porcupine was the best pet of any of the wild animals that I brought home. He loved to curl up with his quills laid down smooth so his belly could be scratched. He would take soda crackers in his paws and eat them, and he loved salted peanuts. However, something bad usually always happens when you make a pet of a wild animal, and in the case of the porcupine, a little 5 year old girl visiting at the neighbors, somehow got two quills in the side of her face while playing with it in our yard. I had to take it to the woods and release it too.

Maybe one of my bigger blunders was when I managed to dodge two dive bombing Golden Eagles while scaling a tall tree to get to their nest, and stole an egg. I brought it home and put it under an old hen chicken that always wanted to set on eggs to hatch them.

When the baby eagle hatched, it began crying in loud screeches. The noises scared the chickens and they all piled up in a corner of the chicken house, killing several of those on the bottom. My grandmother was not a bit proud!

Let me add here, that all my experiences just prove that it is never a good idea to attempt to make a pet from a wild animal.

I have always loved the high back country in the mountains, and always find something very special about being above timberline in the high mountains. There is just something magical about that high mountainous region. I honestly believe that everyone who goes there feels it.

From the time that I was very young, I have often marveled at the small Pica rabbits, or as I knew them from what others I knew that called them Cooney rabbits. I have spent hours watching them scramble among the rocks around lakes above timberline, and listening to their soft almost whistle like bleating talk while I was fishing for the trout in the cold mountain lakes.

The little creatures that actually do somewhat resemble small cottontail rabbits in a way, with small rounded ears; remain busy in the summer months making hay. They will gather grass and other small bits of shrubs then spread the gatherings out on large flat rocks to cure. If a dark cloud suddenly blocks the sun, they will begin to bleat excitedly, while quickly gathering their drying hay, to take it below in the rocks so it will not get rained upon. When the sun comes back out, they again get busy scattering their gatherings around on the top of the large flat rocks.

One thing I have learned about the mountains is that they seem to draw people like a dead carcass draws flies. Most of the people hiking deeper and deeper into the mountains usually carry a gun. One thing about a human carrying a gun in vast wilderness areas, is that they are going to shoot something, if only a can or rock, but for sure they are going to shoot something, and the little, not too timid, Pica rabbits pose too much temptation; to the point that there is only a fraction of them remaining today, compared to what there once was.

Perhaps one of the most amazing and entertaining performances I ever witnessed was a display put on by two golden eagles. I was hunting mountain sheep. I later checked a map to verify the elevation, and as close as I can determine, I was sitting somewhere near 9000 feet.

I had hiked to the top of the mountain, well above timberline, and walked across a vast stretch of the amazing landscape at that elevation. The top of mountains above timberline consists of scant grass, and rocks of various sizes, all splotched with lichens ranging in color from green, yellow, to orange, and red.

Let me take a bit of literary license here for just a paragraph to deviate from the story about the golden eagles to explain another experience that happened that same morning.

Walking across the vast rolling expanse of grass and rock on top of that mountain, I came upon a crack in the large solid granite under base. I had been noticing several smaller cracks, but paid very little attention to any of them, however this was a larger crack, perhaps three feet across, and extending ten or twelve feet long. Peering down into the dark crack, I could not see bottom, so I picked up a softball size piece of granite rock, and dropped it into the crack. I did not hear it hit bottom! So I picked up a much larger rock, perhaps basketball size to drop into the crack. Again, I did not hear it hit bottom! I have no clue how deep that crevice may have been, but I do know I did start paying more attention to the cracks I was seeing, and where I walked.

I walked to the edge of a deep canyon that started on the rim of the area and sat down to glass the area immediately above timber line for mountain sheep. When I sat down, I noticed two golden eagles were circling the same basin. They were circling slowly, right in front of my position, at about the same elevation that I was sitting.

One eagle began to slowly go higher with each circle it made, while the other continued to circle in front of where I was sitting. At first I did not pay a lot of attention to the eagles, just thinking it was interesting that they were circling over the basin at about the same elevation as I was sitting on the rim edge. However as the one eagle kept getting higher and higher, I began to wonder how high it must be flying, and yet it kept going higher and higher.

Glassing for mountain sheep with my 8 power field glasses, I would stop occasionally to look at the eagle through the binoculars, and soon realized that I was having trouble seeing it through the binoculars. I often wonder just how high that eagle must have gone.

There was a stiff, cold breeze blowing where I was sitting, and I had moved twice to find some shelter out of the breeze. I saw a few mule deer, and four elk grazing in the basin below, in clearings in the thick timber, but I had not seen any mountain sheep anywhere. I was beginning to lose interest, and was debating if I would have enough endurance to attempt to walk around the basin and over the far ridgeline to where I would be able to look into yet another different head waters drainage. Being cold, and very tired from the steep long hike I had already made, sitting out of the stiff cold breeze, in a bit of warm sun light, it was easier to procrastinate, and do a bit more looking through the binoculars. It was also easy to pay more attention to the circling eagle.

As I said, I have no idea how high the circling eagle must have gone, but when he topped out, he folded his wings into a power dive position, and dived straight down, just barely missing the eagle that was still slowly circling in front of my position. The cold air made sounds like an approaching missile. The air from the diving eagle made the slower circling eagle wobble and need to quickly adjust its flight. The power diving eagle, did not take its wings out of the dive position, but somehow managed to turn itself back upwards and with all the momentum it again went very high, topped slowly, to curve over and dive again. It barely missed the slower circling eagle both going up and coming down again and that eagle had to catch itself and adjust its flight. Up went the diving eagle again, very high, until the momentum ran out again, then slowly curved over and dived again. It did this perhaps ten or more times, until its final upward momentum, barely came to the same elevation as the slower circling eagle, and at that elevation it opened its wings from the power dive position. Both eagles circled the basin one long wide slow last circle, then went to a prominent point on the opposite side of the basin and perched upon two outstanding large rocks. I remained sitting where I was in total awe, for a long time.

I have no clue what the eagles were doing other than playing, as it was late fall, it was certainly not a mating display. I have never seen anything quite like it since. I often wonder just exactly how high that eagle must have flown, and as I said when I started this story, I had to go home and check maps to get some idea what elevation I was at, then I refuse to even make a guess as to how high the eagle must have flown above that elevation to where I was having trouble keeping it in sight with the eight power binoculars.

Because of my love for the high elevations, above timberline, for about three years, (before you had to draw to get a permit in that area) I hunted for Rocky Mountain Bighorn Sheep. I had several opportunities to kill a decent ram but always passed them up, wanting a bigger one.

Late in the season, when the deep snow pushes everything out of the high mountains, I was hunting mountain sheep where they gather in the winter months. It was also the last weekend of hunting season, and my youngest half brother was with me, hoping to get a big mule deer buck.

I spotted a large ram with seven ewes, high on the side of a mountain, grazing along in a meadow. It would not be an easy climb and the snow was deep, so my half brother elected to search for mule deer on the opposite side of the river canyon that we were in while I attempted to climb to where the sheep were.

The hillside was steep, and deep ravines had washed into the side of the steep hillside. Just as I got to where I could see the mountain sheep, they were moving out of one of these deep sides washed ravines. I got to watch them trickle over the top, from about five hundred yards away, and was surprised at how large that ram really was. I went to the bottom of the ravine, and scaled to the top and again got to see the sheep going over the top of the next deep side washed ravine. So to the bottom I went again, at that point, I got sick to my stomach from all the exercising while pushing myself too hard in the deep snow, and then climbed to the top of that next steep side.

When I eased to the top, where I could look into the next side creek, I could not see any sheep there. Grumbling to myself, thinking that perhaps they had winded me in the fickle high mountain winds that shift direction often, I sat down to rest, under a thick spruce tree, where I could sit upon the branches to keep dry and not have to actually sit on the ground in the snow. As I was sitting there, I suddenly saw a mountain sheep, high above my position coming down the ravine, but on top of the opposite side of the ravine from where I was. I remember thinking at the time that it was a bit odd that the sheep could have made it that far up the mountain on the opposite side of the deep ravine. I could tell that it was a ram, because of the dark coloration. Rocky Mountain Bighorn Rams are always a dark chocolate brown color and ewes are normally grayer, more deer like in coloration. The ram was moving to the top of the other side of the washed ravine that I was looking down into, but was moving through some thick small pine trees. Looking through my scope on my rifle, I could tell that it was a nice ram, but could never get a good look at the horns to tell just exactly how large it really was.

When the sheep finally got to the top of the rim, it moved through some trees, out into the open and stopped there. Problem was it was looking the other direction, away from me, so I could not get a good look at the horns. Mountain sheep have a very irritating habit, which anyone who has ever hunted them will be able to tell you about. They will stop and just stand, often for as much as an hour, in one position, and never move a muscle, which is exactly what that ram did. Just stood there!

After perhaps ten minutes or so of cussing under my breath and talking to myself, I finally decided it must be the big ram I had saw earlier, since mountain sheep are not overly plentiful anywhere, and there were even fewer in this area. I knew when it started to walk again; it would be out of my sight after just a couple more steps down the opposite slope.

I was tired; it had been a long season of climbing in the high mountains. It was the third year I had hunted for mountain sheep without ever having taken a shot at one. My family was not too happy with me hunting mountain sheep every weekend, and my wife and children had made no bones about their disgust with it all. I was playing all this out in my mind, and finally decided it must be the big ram I had saw earlier, and would be a fool not to attempt a shot, even though the range was close to three hundred yards. I brushed some snow away from another tree, sat down, again, used the tree for a rifle rest, and then without a bullet in the chamber, I dry fired on the sheep three times. Finally I loaded a live round, and touched off a shot. With the recoil of the 7mm rifle, I lost sight of the sheep that just seemed to disappear.

Now I really started to cuss myself, because not knowing if I had hit the sheep or not, I would have to go clear to the bottom of the ravine in front of me, and hike clear up the opposite side, to the higher place where the sheep was standing, just to see if I had hit it or not.

Let me take a bit of writer literary license again at this point to tell another story that had led up to this point in time.

Although we had not been raised together, my youngest half brother, Bob, worshiped the ground that I walked on, as only a younger brother can idolize an older brother. When he was very young, he use to attempt to follow me around like a little puppy dog would do. Then when he was sixteen years old, he was in a bad car wreck. He had the side of his head crushed in. While in the hospital, screaming, tied down on the bed, unable to talk well with only slurred cuss words mostly, he would get very upset if a member of the family was not within sight. No one in the family could take listening to him scream for very long, and I ended up being the only one that could stand to be there very long, so I spent three days and nights in that hospital room with him while he screamed.

They had to operate without any anesthetics to remove bone fragments that were pressing inward on his brain, and then he remained tied down screaming, since they do not dare to give anyone with a brain injury any sort of anesthetics for a length of time.

He eventually regained most of his speech and the use of the left side of his body after a couple years.

He had been hunting mule deer on the other side of the river from where I was hunting the mountain sheep, but he had not seen any big buck deer, so he returned to our vehicle and began glassing the hillside where I was. He heard the shot, and saw the ram fall down, and slide down the mountain side, and he saw me start scaling the side of the deep washed draw. So he started rushing up the mountain, and we both got to where the mountain sheep lay, slid up next to a large boulder in the deep snow, about the same time.

I was disappointed to see that the ram was not the big ram that I had been stalking earlier, but that it was a very nice respectable ram. My brother told me that the sheep I had been following were on the same side of the deep washed creek that I was on, only lower, below where I was. I had never seen them.

As I am writing about this, the mounted sheep head is on the wall here in front of my desk.

Let me finish the story by saying that my brother got married that year, and I along with another half brother was the best men at his wedding. He and his wife had a baby girl a year later. He got killed later that same year. The mountain sheep head on my wall will always be a reminder of my brother. Even though I have since seen some bigger mountain sheep in country much easier to hunt them in, I will never hunt mountain sheep again.

Let me tell about one of the black bears that I shot with a bow. While working at the retail/wholesale Firestone Tire and Rubber store in Kalispell, Montana in the early fall, right after the first early snow storm, we were swamped under changing snow tires. They had just hired a young boy about seventeen years old to help with the work overload.

I was busy changing some truck tires on a logging truck outside the rear of the shop, and came through the door with the customer to go into the office to fill out paperwork and collect the money, and passed beside the young man who was putting air into a rear tire of a Farmall tractor tire. The tires are not real large, and they are soft and flexible, but on the old rims, that are usually a bit rusted, the bead does not want to come up easily to seal. He was leaning over the tire pumping air into it, attempting to get one stubborn side to come up and seal. I stopped briefly and told him he better let some of the air out and lubricate that side, before it blew up. He frowned at me, showing his disgust with me telling him what to do. I went on into the office with the customer.

The tire blew up on him, and sent him flying to the fifteen foot ceiling of the steel building. He hit one of the steel beams that supported the thin aluminum ceiling. His upper torso went through the thin roof, and his legs hung limply from the steel rafter. The impact killed him immediately.

Two weeks later, after things settled down a bit from all the commotions of that accident, the store manager hired Rick. Rick was four or five years younger than I was and was about twenty years old. He had polio as a very young boy. He was about six feet tall, stout as a bull, and a bit heavy. Having lost all respect for the people working at the tire store by that time, I took it upon myself to spend some extra time with Rick to teach him some of the proper do and don't things about proper tire mounting, and in that time we had become friends.

Rick was a local boy who had been raised without a father. He wanted to become a hunter and fisherman, but had never had much opportunity to do either one. He was recently married, and quite naive about the world actually in many ways. Strong as a bull, and almost as awkward, he had developed a sense of humor to go with his large frame to make jokes, mostly about himself, and had a kind of wheezing sleeshing way of sucking in air as he giggled.

I was practicing with my bow and arrow, getting ready for

upcoming deer and elk season, and Rick became interested. He bought a bow and some arrows and began practicing with me.

The opening day of archery season we were heading back home from where we had been doing some hunting for elk, and spotted a young black bear grazing on some grass and shrubs in a clearing.

We snuck up to about fifty yards of the bear, which was unaware we were around, and then crawled on our hands and knees to within fifteen yards. I raised up on one knee, when the bear spotted me, I shot the bear, but just as I released the arrow, the bear had started to take a step, and I hit it too far back, in the short ribs.

The bear let out a loud bawl, spun around and bit off the portion of the arrow sticking out of the far side.

I stood up, and was attempting to nock another arrow, when the bear started to charge us. When it did, Rick stood up, and stepped up beside me. The bear, realizing for the first time that there were actually two of us, stopped his charge, and went to a tall pine tree, and started to climb up the tree. It stopped climbing about twenty feet up the tree. It was only about ten yards in front of where we were standing.

Rick hollered at me and said, "Let me shoot em Deacon, can I huh? I have never shot anything with a bow before!"

He had nicknamed me "Deacon" after he saw me with a suit and tie on when I had to attend a regional tire store meeting.

Since I had shot several animals with a bow before, and since it was obvious at that point that it was just supposedly a simple matter of finishing off the bear, I chuckled at him and said, "oh, ok, go ahead."

Excited, and giggling a bit with his sheesh air in breath, Rick quickly drew and shot. He somehow managed to only hit the bear low, in one rear ham.

The bear, literally flew up the tree, putting any smaller squirrel to shame, with the speed and agility as it climbed. It went almost to the top of the tall pine tree in an instant.

Where it finally stopped, it was barely visible. It was impossible to get an arrow through all the branches to get another shot at the bear. So after grumbling, we finally decided that Rick better return to his pickup and get his old 30-30 rifle so we could finish the job, since it would be dark very soon, and I would wait around to see if it would come back down to where I might be able to get another shot at it with the bow.

After it got dark, the bear started to slowly come back down. I could only see it when it would slither around to one side or other of the tree, where it would be sky lined against the lighter sky. I was going to wait until it got down to about twenty feet up, and attempt to get a shot when it was on one side or other of the tree.

Problem was, when it got about to the level I was going to attempt a shot, it suddenly just dropped all the way to the ground, landing with a loud kerplop, right in front of me, maybe ten feet away. I could not see it, but could hear it rustling in the dry leaves, as it moved away towards one side, as I let out a sigh of relief.

Rick smoked cigarettes like a smoke stack, and being Mr. Macho, he always used wooden matches to light his cigarettes. He did not have a flashlight in his pickup, and had been returning to where I was by lighting a match whenever he needed light to see where he was going. I had to holler at him, in the timber to direct him to where I was.

When he got where I was, carrying his old saddle rifle, I told him what had happened. I borrowed a couple of his wooden matches to check the ground where the bear had fallen, for any signs of blood, then followed a faint blood trail to where a log lay. I lit another match, wanting to check the top of the log, to see if there was any blood where they bear would have had to climb over the log, and the bear suddenly rose up right in front of my face, about three feet away.

The loud roar of the rifle going off right beside my head, made me jump, and the match went out. Rick started yelling at the top of his lungs, "Get another match lit Deacon! Get another match lit damn it!"

After awkwardly hurriedly breaking the match top off of three or four matches, I finally managed to get one lit, and we saw that the bear lay dead on the other side of the log.

That was probably the most exciting, stupid bear hunt that I was ever involved with.

II - Destined to Trap

E veryone that I have ever gotten into a deep conversation with has the feeling that they were put on this earth for a reason. Yet, none of us ever know for sure what that reason is. However, with that said, I also believe that way down deep we all know what we need to do. I believe it is ironic how life seems to lead us into a circle, back to what we need to do.

When I was about ten, I remember overhearing a conversation about a government trapper, and later I asked, "You mean people get paid to hunt and trap?" Something about that conversation and the idea seemed to bore deep into my being. I often remember asking that question.

There was a large pile of gravel behind the chicken house where I grew up. It was on the edge of town at that time, and a small swamp bog hole came up near the pile of gravel, and thick brush with quaking aspen trees bordered the water's edge. It was the only place near the house where I could be completely out of sight from my grandmother who was usually knitting or croqueting, while staring out the windows. Whenever I was troubled, I would sit on that pile of gravel. I cried there, got angry and threw rocks hard or just pondered life while I was there. There was always some comfort while being there, as well as some form of wildlife to distract from my troubled mind. Birds flitting in the thick brush, usually a dark colored cat bird that must have had a nest somewhere in the tall rosebushes that grew in a thick clump near the water, frogs, pollywogs, and turtles in the pond, sometimes wild ducks, and now and then a cottontail rabbit near the brush. I spent hours fidgeting with rocks, and small sticks, just sitting on that pile of gravel. I remember dreaming about being paid to hunt and trap while sitting on that pile of gravel.

I was selling Kenworth trucks when my oldest son turned seven years old. I had been on the road all week long, and like always, it was late at night when I returned home. My wife was upset, the boy was asleep on the couch waiting for his dad to come home for his birthday (which I had forgotten about), and the only ones happy to see me come through the door were all the fish in the many aquariums I had made, and a large black housecat that somehow had been adopted into the family. After a bit of confusion, and when my son was put to sleep in his own bed, the wife stomped off to the bedroom, and I sat down on the couch with a flurry of thoughts going through my mind.

Mostly I was thinking about my son, wondering how it could be possible that he was already seven years old, and thoughts about my own life and what I had been doing when I was seven years old. I had been raised in a small rural village, and I roamed and wandered pretty much as I had pleased at that age. My son, on the other hand was being raised in the large growing town of Billings, Montana. While we lived across the street from one of the largest city parks, we dared not let the children go to the park alone, because of all the bad things that happen in city parks. I did not sleep that night. I went to work the next day and turned in my resignation.

Two weeks later, I was loading my family and belongings to move to the small town of Jordan, Montana. I opened a small retail tire store.

People in the trucking industry thought that I was crazy and that something had snapped, (perhaps they were correct, as I have often wondered about that decision myself) because I had been quite successful selling large trucks. The Kenworth factory called and offered me a job, as did several other retail truck dealerships. Two

even came to visit, thinking they could talk some sense into my head, but I hung on in Jordan.

Being young and in very good health, I worked in the tire store all day, then helped butcher livestock in the evenings for a good friend who owned the butcher shop and grocery store. Two nights of the week and on the weekends I would tend bar. When trapping season opened, I began running a trapline at night

Furs drying in tire shop in Jordan, Montana.

or early mornings, and on the weekends.

The home that I had rented did not have a garage or any out buildings, so I did my skinning in the tire shop, and would put the hides on stretchers and hang them about in the shop. When sheep men would come into the shop for tires, and see the coyotes and fox skins hanging around, they would beg me to trap on their property.

One thing led to another and then one day one of the county commissioners, who I dealt with often about tires, said that the county was considering hiring a part time trapper to assist with coyote control work in the county, and asked if I may be interested in the job.

The tire shop had been growing slowly, but steadily, and I was actually at a crossroads in that business. I needed to either borrow money to expand my inventory to keep up with the business, or start losing business. I was not overly fond of the tire shop business, but it was something I knew a good deal about, having worked while in college at a large gas station that sold a lot of tires, then having worked for BF Goodrich for a year after dropping out of college to support my growing family. Being able to trap full time was a dream, but now it seemed a possibility, as I could work for the county in the summer months then trap for fur in the winter months.

It was not an easy decision, and my wife did not like the idea, because of the lack of security, but something deep inside would not let me make any other decision. So I closed the tire shop and became a full time year round trapper.

I have never regretted most of this change in my life, as both of my boys today have their Doctorate degrees, and my daughter has a Master's degree, and they are all happily married with children of their own, and I am still a full time year-round trapper, even though the marriage did not eventually fare so well.

When I started to write this, I thought about the multitudes of people that I have met through the years while trapping, and thinking that I needed to write something about many of them. However as I begin to start this, I also realize very quickly that I will never be able to include more than just a very few of the real, for a lack of better word description, "characters" that I have met.

Frank Morgan is on the right, on the left is the traveling fur buyer.

To start, let me quickly just mention one old sheep herder with a large family that lived in a very isolated area. He called his coffee and chewing tobacco "spirits." He always wanted me to stop and have a cup of spirits [coffee]. He rarely had any fresh coffee. He never changed the grounds in the coffee pot, just added some more. You did not drink his coffee, you chewed it. Yet, he insisted so hard that I must have coffee, so that I managed to force myself to sit and chew my way through several cups at different times over a few years, while enjoying the conversations with him and his family.

There is another old sheep herder and his wife with a large family who looked tired and bent over, always appearing older than he really was, but whose wife was always spry and full of spunk.

Another unique individual is a horse and cattle rancher whose father had bred and raised the famous bucking horse "Trails End." He still maintains the blood lines today. Even though a Polio survivor who has a bad arm because of the disease, he spent a life on the ranch while becoming an authority on war survivors and wars in general. If I started to mention his family members, I would almost have to write a book about each one to give them justice for the characters they truly are, and were.

Another character and a good friend was the foreman for a large ranch that was only one of three large ranches. He is often gruff, and always straight to the point of things, to the extent that many people are very cautious in his presence. He was a bit reluctant to allow me on the ranch at first to do predator control work. In time, we became very good friends. Over the years, I caught or shot many coyotes on that property.

An endless number of trappers that I have had the opportunity to meet and a few that have become good friends that I probably should write about, but I will only mention a very few here to describe how their influence helped change my life. Yet, there are men like old Jim Jones who was friends with Bill Nelson, and knew George Good when he was young. If I started to include some of Jim's family members it would lead me into more trappers that I have became friends with. The list goes on and on and include people like Laurie Jones (now Laurie Jones Woolson--well known as simply "the Cat" on the trapperman forum), Jackie Malone (a real character for certain that I could write several stories about) John Rockwood, who is now the current President of the New York Trappers association, Tom Whiting (Grit) the modern day squeaker marketer, Cindy Seff, who is in the National Trappers Hall of Fame for all the work she continually does to promote trapping, Kyle Kaatz, the editor/co-owner of Trappers World magazine, and believe I will stop there, as this list could go on longer than the book itself is intended to be. If I continued, I would also have to include several of the trap line students that have paid me for trap line lessons. So let me just go back again and tell about a few characters that have played major roles in my life at times.

There was an old gentleman by the name of Frank Morgan with a reputation of being a very good coyote trapper living in Jordan, Montana when I moved there. I made it a point to look him up and introduce myself. We became quite good friends. Frank was in his late 60's when I met him, and he had a private predator control program working with several of the largest sheep producers in the county. When I went to work for the county, we would often work together attempting to stop some depredation by coyotes.

Frank was a very colorful character in many ways. Sort of gruff and straight to the point, but with a "wisened" mannerism. If you could get him started, when he had the time, he loved to tell stories about himself and his brother when they were young, hunting coyotes and chasing mountain lions with hounds, in an almost excited tone of voice, and using expressions that would hold a listener's interests. Frank always had a large old hound dog tied up beside his trailer home.

While I was still in the tire shop, Frank Morgan stopped by to ask if I had any extra coyote urine that he might be able to purchase. I did not, so he asked if I would be willing to help him drive to Circle, Montana, which was only sixty miles away, and get some urine from the government trapper that lived there. He said George Good had coyotes penned up and always had coyote urine. I had heard many stories about George Good, and knew that he was the best coyote trapper in Montana, and was employed by the government ADC program at that time. It didn't take me more than a few minutes to throw things around and shut down the tire shop, so I could make the trip with Frank.

When I was very young, and first attempting to catch a few animals, all the old trappers that I knew about were very quiet and standoffish, refusing to talk about trapping, and even getting upset if asked anything about it. In that time frame, most of the older trappers made some extra income trapping to help them get through the Depression, and trapping was all a big secret. A few of them would even get upset at me when I showed up with my skunk skins to sell at the local livestock feed store, demanding to know where I had caught the skunks, and then quickly warning me not to go trapping where they were trapping.

I considered myself very lucky to have befriended Frank Morgan, and even though he would not tell me much about how to trap, we did talk about trapping often. Frank was mostly from the old school of coyote trappers, using old rusty traps, set in trails that the coyotes would use, or in front of a few drops of coyote urine placed on sagebrush. Frank used his old hound to locate where he would want to place his urine to set a trap. Often he would just place a trap where his hound had urinated.

Meeting George Good was like a breath of fresh air. I was expecting a gruff, closed mouth, hardened individual who more than likely guarded his secrets. Instead, George proved to be a very friendly individual who was almost thrilled that two trappers had came to visit. His wife, Faye, was just as friendly and bubbling with happy enthusiasm that we had come to visit them.

Faye Good put up all the fur after George skinned the animals. They showed us the long string of dry fox and coyote hides that were finished. There were a lot of coyote and fox furs, and it was obvious she did a beautiful job. She washed the furs in an old washing machine, did an excellent job of sewing any holes, as well as combing the dry furs. In time I would learn that she was also a very good coyote trapper. (Several years later, after George died an untimely death from a heart attack, she would take over the private predator control operation that George started after becoming disillusioned with the federal ADC program, and she did an excellent job of running that operation.)

George took us out to the coyote shed to show us the coyotes he had in pens over trays that sloped towards a trough draining into a bucket to catch the coyote urine. He began apologizing that two of the wire pens needed to be rebuilt since the floor was starting to rust and were about ready to break. He said he had new wire, but had been waiting until the weekend when he could get a ranch kid to help him cut and bend the wire, as it was just too awkward for one person to do easily by himself. George then said that he was a bit concerned that maybe the young sheep rancher's son would not show up, since he was a bit wild and not always as reliable as he could be. I quickly told him that I could come and help on Sunday if he wouldn't mind. He seemed a bit shocked at first, and then said that wouldn't be necessary as it was quite a drive, but I insisted. Later when he told Faye that I was going to come help him build coyote pens, she demanded that I come early enough to have dinner with them.

The day of helping George build coyote pens began a long,

much valued, lasting friendship. It was also the day that I met Ward Witte. Ward became a very good trapper and a friendship developed between us that has lasted to this day.

All of this was taking place in the early 70's when long hair fur prices were just beginning to steadily climb higher. That fall, Craig O'Gorman came to the area to trap. He heard about me through the family where he was staying and through George Good. He came to the tire shop to visit, and later to my home for supper, and another friendship developed that has persevered the trial and tribulations of time to this day.

Looking back on it all now, I realize how fortunate I was to be trapping at that time in the right place. How fortunate could one man be, to live where he could befriend some of the greatest trappers of the time?

I went on the trap line with all of these men, learning something from each and they went with me on my trap lines. I spent countless hours talking trapping with all of them.

George Good talked about coyotes continually; so much so that it became a bit of a joke with the rest of his family. They had made a bet; to see how long it would be before George did not say the word, "coyote" in a sentence. I do not remember who won the bet, but I do remember that they affectionately, laughingly, told the story, saying it was exactly 20 something minutes. George did not deny it; he just stared at the floor and shrugged his shoulders, then changed the subject—to coyotes of course.

My very first experiences doing predator control work was certainly a learning experience and more than a few lessons about frustrations. Since old Frank Morgan had the reputation of being the best coyote man in Garfield County, Montana, and we had established a friendship, I did my very best to work with him, and delicately prove to him that I was not trying to compete with his operations.

Probably because of his age, and no doubt because of his many years of experience with sheep ranchers, Frank loved to hunt coyotes from an airplane. He would use me to do what can only be called grunt work on the ground while the airplane took credit for the kills. I would spend several days walking and searching for

Seeing a coyote bouncing as it tries to escape when I pull up to one in a trap is a thrill that is much more than a simple accomplishment. Staring into the cold yellow eyes of a coyote always seems to make something transpire between us.

It is impossible to look into the eyes of a coyote without realizing that not only are the lights on, but someone is home too.

coyote tracks and droppings to figure where the coyotes were living, then go to the area before daylight to blow a large siren to make the coyotes howl. When the airplane would arrive, shortly after full sun up, I would be on a high hill where they could find me, and I would point to where the coyotes had answered the siren. If the coyotes got into some timber, or worse, crawled into a hole in the ground somewhere, the airplane would direct me to the area to either chase the coyotes out so they could shoot them, or I would have to dig them from the holes in the ground.

Many times I would set traps for the killer coyotes in the general area that I had tracked them to, only to have the airplane arrive a day or so later and kill the coyotes.

Summer trapping is much different than winter time trapping, because of the heat, bugs, mice, scavenger birds, and domestic livestock that have been put out on the open rolling range, limiting where traps can be used, and the type sets and lures that can be productive. I caught some coyotes in areas too rough for the airplanes to do much good, and learned daily while getting little sleep at night and sweat soaked my clothes during daytime hours.

I had high hopes that after spending the summer months getting to know ranchers and searching vast areas of landscape, that when furs got good in the late fall, my fur trapping would be easier

My oldest son Clint and I with a few frozen furs to sell when buyer came to town.

and better. I soon learned that many sheep ranchers that wanted me around all summer did not want me trapping once furs were sellable. Cattle ranchers were even worse, because the hired men always wanted to trap or hunt for the furs when they got prime. I was told often that every penny the hired help could make from furs was one penny they would not ask the ranchers for. To begin with, my winter fur trapping was not as easy as I had hoped for. So I kept my job tending bar at night.

Victor Trap Company was the only company making traps at that time, and they only made one trap that was decent for catching coyotes. I did not have enough money to buy more than just a few of the expensive #3N traps, so I began tinkering with cheaper #3 traps, by reversing the loose jaw, and welding a wire on the inside contact edge of each jaw.

Today, you can order traps directly from the companies that make traps that have been laminated. Although certainly not the first to have laminated traps, I do believe that I was the first to write about the use of laminated jaw traps in a method book, which would eventually lead to the companies that make traps offering the laminations for sale.

I also went to the small local hardware store and bought some heavy cable, which I then took apart strand by strand, so I could make a snare from each strand of the heavier cable. I have no idea how many hours I spent twisting and untwisting cable into various fashions of resemblance to a workable snare, but soon just made a knot that would close upon itself to lock tight.

After describing the knot, and drawing diagrams about how to make it workable in a methods book, I was to later win the National Trappers Association's "Pioneer Award" for the method books about snares and the locking knot. It would be several more years, and a few books more, and countless numbers of trapper association demonstrations to show proper use of traps and snares, before I would be inducted into the National Trapper's Association's "Hall of Fame" for the work devoted to improve trapping.

Looking back again on it all now, I have to sometimes wonder why I didn't just give up on the whole thing. I admit that I wanted to prove something to everyone as well as myself, that I could do

Typical coyote killed lamb, with only the tender parts eaten.

it and make it all work somehow. However, as those thoughts creep in, I know deep inside that it was always my love for the outdoors and the need to be in contact, up close, with nature that made me so bull headed stubborn. Then too, there is just something about coyotes that I probably will never be able to explain, not fully understanding it myself, but even yet today, it seems that the more I learn about them, the more I seem to feel a need to always know just a bit more.

Old Frank Morgan told it in his colorful mannerism a different way. He would go into a long story about a college professor that figured if an old reprobate like Frank Morgan could make money trapping, he should be able to get rich at it. So being a professor, he started figuring out how many acres a coyote would travel over their normal six to eight mile travels, and then he broke that down into inches. He measured a coyote's foot and multiplied it by four, and measured the pan on a trap to figure out how many traps he would need. Then he began to figure possibilities and probabilities. At this point in the story, Frank would throw both arms up in mock jester at imitating the supposed frustrated professor, who would suddenly announce in the spring, after not setting one trap all winter long, that his pile of papers proved that catching a coyote in a foot hold trap was all but impossible to do.

An old established fur buyer would come to the small town of Jordan about once a month to buy furs, and he would meet people at Frank's trailer home. He would buy the animals whole and frozen. He was very colorful, shrewd, and interesting. When I went to his place of business in North Dakota, I learned a lot about skinning animals and handling the fur when it was skinned. Just watching them flesh raccoons was a valuable lesson in itself, but seeing how they skinned frozen animals was a valuable lesson as well.

After more than 30 years of year-round trapping, mainly for coyotes, there have been many interesting experiences. Many are forgotten until something happens, or someone else brings something up to remind me about some incident or other. One experience I will remember forever however.

I believe if you talk to any trapper with much experience, they will tell you that sometimes things become very personal between the trapper and a particular animal. I was supposed to be working, doing coyote depredation control, and it was suppose to be just a job, but this particular coyote and I became very personal. I believe that coyote knew me and my habits better than I did.

A coyote family had moved into a very rough canyon of deep, straight drop off sides, and water washed creeks. The more sloping ground that drained into these deep washed creeks was covered with tall thick juniper cedar brush, and an occasional taller pine tree scattered about along the high sides. The cedars and pine trees slowly gave way to tall sagebrush covered slopes nearing the steep drop off sides of the creeks. The very bottom of these steep sided creeks were mostly just flat sun baked mud that contained brittle grease wood scattered around between clumps of thick chokecherry bushes. The many, small, deep drainages eventually drained into two main creeks that joined together. It was very good wildlife habitat, providing home to deer, a few antelope, many jackrabbits and cottontail rabbits, as well as badgers and a few raccoons and bobcats. The ranchers that owned the land, as well as the neighbors, all raised sheep, and the coyotes began leaving the rough canyon and killing lambs on three different ranches.

Because the area was so difficult to even walk in, I spent many hours attempting to figure the area out, and locate where the coyotes may possibly have a den.

Some friends had given my children a pup border collie. Since my wife worked at the local hospital, and my children were in school for most of the day, there was no one around to supervise the ambitious little devil that would become bored and start chewing things up. So it became my daily task to take the dog with me.

Walking along the top edge of one steep drop off drainage, the dog and I were searching for coyote tracks. The dog loved to chase the chipmunks and cottontail rabbits as he roamed ahead of me. I always carried my rifle, just in case I may get a chance to spot the coyotes, but was unprepared without a cartridge in the chamber when the dog suddenly came running back out of some cedar juniper brush with a coyote in hot pursuit behind him. Everything happened very quickly, and very close, perhaps twenty yards in front of me. The dog ran to my side, and the coyote pulled up when he saw me, stopped briefly, then slowly trotted back into the tall cedars. I loaded a shell into the chamber and tried in vain to encourage the dog to pursue the coyote.

The next day I again returned near the area, at daylight, sitting down at a vantage place that I had located the day before. I had the dog with me. My intentions were to attempt to call the coyotes, and use the dog as a decoy to distract their attentions. It worked entirely too well and way too fast again. Two adult coyotes came bounding in flying leaps over the tall sagebrush almost before I had finished my first squeak on the hand held predator call. The dog began barking, and the coyotes headed towards us entirely too fast to get a shot. I barked myself, and threw my baseball cap towards the closest coyote in an attempt to stop it. When it jumped backwards and stopped briefly, I shot the large female coyote. The second coyote veered away quickly, returning back to the tall cedar bushes.

The very old female coyote was wet, with swollen teats and full of milk. Later after I drug her from the rough canyon, and loaded her into my pickup and took her to show the closest rancher, I cut her open to count the scars on her uterus, to find out how many pups she had. She showed 8 distinct scars.

It had taken me almost thirty days to kill the coyote from the time the coyotes had first killed lambs. Since the coyotes had been killing on several different locations and three different ranches, the problems had been reported to every predator control agent around the locality. Frank Morgan had flown the area searching for the coyotes, as well as the district supervisor for the federal ADC program. I knew the den must be very close to where I shot the coyote, and I reported it to Frank Morgan, as well as the district supervisor. Frank flew the area the next day, and killed another adult coyote in the bottom of one of the steep creeks. He called me and told me exactly where it was laying, so I could go retrieve it to show to the local ranchers. We both just assumed that it was the male coyote, however when I found it, it proved to only be another yearling female coyote, a baby sitter so to speak. However as I was walking into the area, to retrieve the dead coyote, I spotted three large fluffy pup coyotes sitting near the head of one of the steep washed creeks. The banks of the head of the steep creek had caved away, causing a large area of rubble from the jumbled, fallen, large sod clumps. There were holes everywhere in the rubble. A perfect place for a coyote den, but impossible to figure out where the pups may be scattered in the many different holes.

When George Good heard about everything, in the late afternoon, he volunteered to come over and help me locate the pups. When we finished, way after dark, we both knew we had not gotten all the pups. There were just too many holes everywhere to search things out completely.

Hoping what coyotes had been killed was going to stop the lamb killing in the area, soon proved to be a false wish. Three days later, the killing started again, much more seriously than it had been before. Where the coyotes had been killing one to three lambs for food before, the old male coyote now began killing for revenge, and would often kill as many as eight or more lambs, never eating from any of them. The worst I ever saw, was one night he actually killed eighteen lambs, in a straight row, spaced about twenty to thirty yards apart.

I attempted to call the male and shoot it, many times, without ever seeing him. I set traps on every possible likely travel way that I would locate, and I did manage to catch one yearling male coyote in a trap, but the killing just continued, nightly.

Thirty long long days later, the state helicopter came to the county, and we flew the rough canyon, searching hard for the male coyote with no success. A small rain storm started to move into the area as we were leaving the canyon. I spotted the coyote running hard ahead of us. Hard gusty winds had came up with the storm, and was blowing directly into our face as we attempted to catch up to the fleeing coyote, who was actually gaining distance between us as we struggled to keep sight of it in the rain while the pilot struggled to fly directly into the hard winds. We caught up to him, just as he was jumping down into one of the steep sided washed creeks, and I got off a very quick shot, just as he jumped into the creek. He went down hard, but before the pilot could get the helicopter turned around in the hard winds and rain, the coyote managed to get up and disappear. We landed and searched on foot for awhile but the cold rain started coming harder and we had to abandon the search.

After all the effort and a long hot summer of attempting to kill the coyote, I evidently did kill him, as it never was seen again, nor did it kill any more lambs. I just never got my hands on him. With him dead, and no longer protecting them, I caught three large pup coyotes in traps that had been set for the killer.

Fur prices had been going up steadily, and I had high hopes to make some serious money when winter came, as I would no longer be working for the government, but would be on my own fur trapping again. Best laid plans of mice and men! Mother Nature had other plans!

It started snowing hard on the 8th of October 1978, dumping only roughly six or seven inches of heavy wet snow, then the temperature plunged below zero. It snowed another five or six inches, and temperature went down some more. Then it warmed clear into the upper 40 degree range for two days, and everyone had high hopes that the melting snow would disappear, only to again have the temperatures drop suddenly and start to snow very hard, dumping over two feet of snow. Then it warmed again for two days, followed by another cold snap with additional snows. The warm stretches caused ice on top of the snow each time it got cold and snowed again. The ice was acting like reinforcement rebar in concrete. Regular snow plow equipment could not move the snow. Livestock that were stuck in open range could not be reached to be fed by ranchers with 4 wheel drive tractors. The wind blew hard every day and night, drifting any loose snow into huge drifts anywhere the wind did not touch. The problem was that the wind would blow from the Northwest for five or six days, then switch and come directly from the Southeast for several days, only to again reverse itself once more. Snow drifts were very hard, and collected anywhere there might have been any shelter from the relentless cold winds. The eleventh of November the temperatures again dropped well below zero, and would not again get above zero until very late March. Clouds hung low, and would spit light cold snow that was probably only frost layers each night. With the fog, blowing snow and frost, the land became consumed in a major whiteout. In a whiteout of this proportion, it is impossible to turn around and see your own tracks, much less where you are going in front of you.

Every Caterpillar dozer owned by construction companies was hired to attempt to open a few roads and get to some ranchers and/or their livestock.

During this time, I had followed road crews to a rim of land that dropped eventually to a river many miles below and away from the rim. From the rim down, erosion had occurred for many years, and formed a vast area known only as the breaks, consisting of steep sided creeks with tall trees in the bottoms, and smaller tributaries on the sides lined with juniper cedars and tall sagebrush that was home to a lot of wildlife. With snowshoes, I had hiked into the rough terrain to hang some snares for predators in the thick juniper cedar clumps, and managed to put out five steel foothold traps on a couple of windswept ridge tops. I would check these sets whenever I could get to the rim on the plowed road, by walking into the breaks with the snowshoes.

While in high school, I hurt my knee in an athletic event. It seemed that the extreme cold always made that knee act up, by locking up. I could not bend it when it would lock, and it would not straighten either, tending to lock when my leg was partially bent. If I would just sit down, and not put any pressure on the leg, the knee would usually finally relax and be alright after an hour or so. I tell you all this so that I can relate a spiritual event that burned a memory into my mind that I will carry forever and sometimes often relive in my dreams at night.

To shorten this story, let me just say that when I parked my vehicle on the rim of the breaks to hike down and check my snares and traps, it was well below zero. I had hopes that it may warm up later in the afternoon, but it started to snow instead. On my return trip back up the hills, out of the breaks, I stepped on a downed tree limb that was hidden just beneath the surface of the snow. The snowshoe slipped back and sideways on that hidden slick pole when I put my weight on that leg, causing me to take a hard tumble in the deep snow. When I attempted to stand up, the knee locked up, solid! I could not make that leg straighten. Walking in deep snow was difficult enough before, but became almost impossible to do hobbling along with one leg that did not work correctly. I had to sort of stretch the shortened leg to gain a small step, then take as long a step as possible from a half slouched position with the good leg. I was sliding the snowshoes through the loose snow on top of the hard drifted snow underneath as I moved. Often I would fall through the crusted top layer of hard drifted snow, when the snow shoes were not large enough to fully support my weight, and getting out of the depression was extremely difficult and painful with the locked up knee. The pain and extra exertion tired me out very quickly, even though I was in very good physical shape at the time. I still had almost three miles to go uphill in order to reach my parked vehicle. I think that may be the longest three miles I ever walked.

I was bundled in heavy clothing with long handle underwear, felt lined packs, heavy wool shirt, beaver skin vest, and a heavy parka. I had been hurrying as much as possible when I first started down into the breaks, and as far as I had returned before I fell. I can't say that I had worked up a sweat, as it was much too cold for that, but I had heated up my body with all the exertions. Struggling to walk uphill in the half slouched position was making me sweat under all my clothes, even though the temperatures started to fall drastically when I was about half way up the steepest part of the hike.

I was played out, and it was starting to get dark. Since I could not even stand on one leg without causing severe pain in the knee of the other leg, I would stop to rest by sitting on my haunches. I was taking a long break, breathing hard and tasting the cold air as it burned my throat and lungs while inhaling. For the first time, I was seriously beginning to worry that I may not be able to make it to the top of the rim.

While sitting on my haunches pondering my fate, the relentless winds, just suddenly quit blowing. It was not unusual to have the hard winds die down shortly after dark, almost like it was taking a break before starting to blow again on the night shift.

In today's world of hustle and bustle, I am not too certain very many people ever really actually experience total quiet, or certainly not for more than a minute or two at the most. However sitting there on my haunches in that cold, when the wind stopped blowing, a quiet engulfed the land like no words could begin to describe. It was a muffling all encompassing clutching quiet. As I sat there on my haunches drinking in the quietness, suddenly below and slightly to one side of my position a lone coyote howled a long eerie single howl that someway seemed to break the trance of the deep quiet cold air.

I know I will never forget that long lone single howl. When I heard the howl, I turned towards that direction, and started to slowly stand up, attempting to get a glimpse of the animal, without realizing that I was doing so. Somehow, I managed to stand completely upright before I realized that I had. The whole experience will never be forgotten!

From that point, it was an easy hike to go the last mile to my vehicle, and from that day, until I would have to eventually get it operated on, I could always manage to get the knee to unlock and to straighten the leg, by crouching on my haunches, relaxing, and standing slowly. To this day, there is just something almost magical, and spiritual about that whole experience that I will probably never completely understand.

I believe I could almost write a complete book about the stories of that winter if I went into details about everything I remember.

When I could no longer get into the country to trap, I started to write my very first trapping methods book, "Predator Trapping Problems and Solutions." My wife was upset with me, asking who did I think I was, and telling me that I was wasting time, and that I needed to go somewhere to look for a job that I could make some money doing something more productive.

Meanwhile, the cold, deep snow, whiteout winter seemed to drag on and on, killing livestock and wildlife alike.

The family that owned the land, and the sheep that had been killed by the killer coyote that I just described, had become good friends. Pop Whiteside, as he was affectionately known by everyone in the area, was in his early 80's and he had two married sons. Work was the only thing that any of them ever knew. The youngest boy, Jim, had just recently married a local girl, and during the middle of the winter she had a baby that had to be flown to Denver, Colorado for emergency open heart surgery. The older son, Charles, called me and told me the news. Knowing that Charles would not be able to handle the work load while Jim was away, I volunteered to come help them until he could return.

I was barely able to make it to the ranch in my four wheel drive pickup, only because the roads had recently been plowed, but that night it snowed hard again with cold winds blowing steadily, closing every road that had been plowed open. What I had anticipated would only be a week or so at the most, turned into almost two months before I could get back out, or Jim could get back home.

I enjoyed that time with the Whiteside family. The work was hard, but usually interesting. When I arrived, all the livestock had been moved close to the ranch headquarters. However getting to hay yards was next to impossible, as most of the hay had been placed in the normal winter pastures. There were a few real old loose hay stacks near the headquarters, and they were used both as shelters from the cold winds for sheep and cattle, as well as emergency feed. Supplement feeds, stored in grain bins, were available, but feeding it in the deep snow wasted about as much as the livestock could find to eat. Even though the livestock were no more than a half mile away, four wheel drive tractors were needed to plow a trail to them and clear a feeding area every day, but each time that was done, the incessant blowing winds would fill the plowed trails with fresh harder packed snow drifts, so after a couple of days a new trail would need to be plowed open. A few livestock just quit trying, and laid down to die. Most of the rest had a very tired look about them, as they stumbled about in the deep snows, or lay down whenever possible, usually on the fresh hay that was offered to them for food.

To add insult to injury, the sheep came down with a disease that started to cause them to abort the lambs, so we would have to run them into the large shed about once a week then vaccinate each one. Manhandling over a thousand sheep is very difficult, hard work.

When I was young, my grandmother raised me. When she broke her leg and was confined to the wheelchair, I was eight years old. My grandmother owned a few chickens, and those chickens and the eggs they laid were often our only source of income, and they became my responsibility. I hated shoveling out the small chicken house, as it was full of little red chicken mites that would get on me and even though they did not bite, they would drive me crazy crawling around. The dust and smells were not very enjoyable. When I left home, I vowed to never, ever shovel out another chicken house the rest of my life. About the third week at the Whiteside ranch, they decided that I should clean out the turkey shed. Boy did I talk to myself and bite my tongue. While I shoveled the dusty mess, I kept repeating to myself, over and over, "Pedersen, it ain't chickens!"

Another incident that happened while herding sheep in the large tin shed, will be remembered for a couple reasons: embarrassment probably as much as anything else, and also because it was only the second time in my life that I was close to being knocked unconscious. The short version is simply that while attempting to push some sheep through a small gateway, I was bent over with my arms outstretched attempting to shoo the sheep. An old ewe turned around and jumped, straight into me, butting heads. It knocked me to my knees and made me see flashing lights. Shirley Whiteside, Charles's wife, began to laugh uncontrollably, causing others in the shed to laugh as well, even me once I regained my composure a bit.

Since my fur take was very small that winter, the wages that the Whiteside family later paid me for my time was much appreciated. When the weather finally broke, and I could return to where I had put snares and traps, I found twelve frozen coyotes that I managed to thaw out and skin to sell the hides. Since good Montana coyotes were averaging better than 80 dollars at that time, the fur check made a big difference. It often seems that somehow God always provides a way, if a person just keeps going, doing the best that they know how to do.

When spring finally did arrive, dead antelope and deer lined the barrow ditches of every roadway that had been plowed in the winter. I knew it had been happening, but it was not as apparent as it was in the spring. Early in the winter most plant eating animals had moved to the tops of the high hills, where winds blew the snow off, as that was the only place they could locate any food. As the winter drug along, everything edible had been eaten down to the roots on the tops of hills. The hard deep snow drifts had the animals penned on the top of the hill where they were. When a road had been plowed for vehicle traffic, the stranded animals would get into the road searching for a way to go anywhere to get away from the deep snow and seek food. When a vehicle came along, the animals were forced to get off the road into the hard snow. Many did not have the strength to return back onto the road to continue their travels, and they died there. When the roads were plowed again, those animals were buried. In the spring of the year, it looked like someone had traveled the roads with a machine gun and just killed everything within sight on the edge of every road.

The next winter was almost as bad as that first one, only it started later, and subsided sooner in the spring. My overall fur take was again short that winter, but it was much better than the year before had been, and I did make enough money to pay all expenses and have a bit left over. Yet, everything seemed quite uncertain, and when the government offered me a part time job in Ekalaka, Montana, doing predator control work, with a carrot dangling in front about the possibility of a year around full time position if things worked out, I took them up on the offer.

To give you a bit more of an understanding about how deep the snow had been that winter; when I examined the home during the early spring that I eventually bought in Ekalaka, I had no idea what color the house was, but I could tell it had a very good roof. I walked up the side of the large snowdrift on one end of the house to the roof. The hard winds had blown the roof clear.

The first year in Carter County, I did very well on fur in the winter, as red fox were very plentiful, as were bobcats, mink, muskrats, and beaver. Coyotes were not overly plentiful, and only to be found in the very roughest of terrains where the airplane was unable to eliminate them. I balked a bit the next year when the government did offer me a full time year around position, but made the mistake of taking the position, knowing that supervisors were aging and about to retire. What I had not anticipated was that the supervisor changes would be unbearable so I ended up quitting after my first year of full time work. The local sheep ranchers came to me and asked what they could do to keep me there, so I put together a proposition, and remained there for another 25 years working under a private contract.

I suppose I should have learned something from my experience with the government about supervisors being replaced, as all the people on the board of directors of the Sheep and Cattle Growers Association in Carter County eventually grew older and were replaced, and as that transpired, no one was left that remembered how things had started originally. As I am writing this today, I now live in the state of Georgia, again doing private predator control work under contract with a private individual. The only thing about life that is for certain is that something is always going to change!

I messed around with predator calls since I was a teenager and have called many animals. Since no one else had ever used a predator call where I lived as a teenager, wild magpie birds would come flocking to the sounds. I loved to torment the smart devils with the Burnham Brothers Predator calls. The experience with the Border collie dog convinced me that use of a dog as a decoy while

Ekalaka City Main street after a bit of snow removal had been done.

calling had a lot of merit. However, he wanted to herd, not hunt, and he did not have a very good nose for trailing.

A few years later, I drove into a sheep rancher's headquarters. The rancher was also a hound hunter and owned several large hounds that he just allowed to roam. As the dogs came barking and bounding towards my pickup when I pulled in front of the home, a small looking hound that appeared to be an adult caught my attentions. When I asked about the breed, the hardened old rancher just laughed a deep belly chuckle. He went on to tell the story of what he thought was his birth control dog. It was a small, mean dachshund that someone from town had given him. It was too mean to keep in the city limits. He said the little dog was so mean that all the large slower hounds were scared of it. He also would chase away the male hounds when one of the female hounds came into cycle. He then said it worked well for two years, but evidently the small dog had found the milk stool, because one of the female hounds produced a litter of pups that were half dachshund. While we both chuckled, I told him if it ever happened again, I would like one of the pups.

One week later, the rancher's large frame filled my doorway

when my wife and daughter were home alone, and he handed my daughter a small pup that was half dachshund and half blue tick hound. With his deep soft way of chuckling he told them to tell me that if I did not like the dog, it had a large dark spot on each side that could be used for a target.

I had just recently shot and killed a five month old dog that my wife had brought home, thinking it may be something I could use on the trapline. It was a cross of half German Shepherd and half Doberman. It was the meanest darn thing I had ever been around, and almost un-trainable in any way. After it had chased sheep, earlier that morning, I had chased him down and reprimanded him, and less than an hour later it had again chased sheep, and caught an old ewe as I came over the hill. I just grabbed my rifle and out of anger, shot the dog.

Remembering that I had just shot one dog, the old rancher's comments about a target on each side of the little pup had stirred up both women, and they both glared at me when they told me the story and quickly added that I dare not to shoot it.

I am going to have to ask the readers indulgence a bit here, as I attempt to explain the many experiences with the blue-tick dachshund dog, because this could drag along awhile.

I named the dog George, after George Good. I told George Good, it was so he would become a good coyote dog.

Poor George with his lineage was not sure if he wanted to be a hound or a dash hound. He had a very good trailing nose, but would want to crawl into every hole he chased something into.

He had the bawl of a hound, and would want to trail and bawl on a fresh scent trail. Most of all my previous experiences with hounds had never been good, as it seemed a person would listen to them bawl out of ear range and then spend the next several days looking for the dog. I did not want that, as I did not have the time to run around searching for a dog.

I had moved an old weigh scale shed into my back yard, and had recently made three pens to put on a rack in the shed, above a tin tray to catch coyote urine. I had put three half grown pup coyotes in the pens. I used both some urine and droppings from those coyotes to teach George what we were searching for. He caught on quickly, and my boys would often ask George where the coyotes were. He would run to the shed and begin to bark and howl.

George had entirely too much ambition, so I would dump him out of the pickup and make him run to tire him out, and if he would locate anything to do with coyotes, I would make over him and tell him what a good dog he was. Whenever he would run over the hill bawling like a large hound, I would drive off and leave him. He was young enough that he panicked when he realized that I was not following and he was all alone, so he would eventually come looking for the pickup. However, he was smart and soon knew just about how far he could trail something and still come back and locate the pickup. The more he grew, the farther he would go, and when he was a year old, it was becoming a problem.

George had been small when we got him, and when I first started taking him with me, I just let him ride on the seat of the pickup next to me. Since it was just him and I riding around daily, he soon showed another trait. He would get jealous if anyone else got into the pickup truck with us, and sat in his seat.

I called up a pair of coyotes and managed to shoot them both when George was only about four months old. He was a good decoy, as he searched for mice and rabbits in front of where I was sitting when I was calling. When he barked and growled at the dead coyotes, I teased him with them, pushing them towards him, and pulling them back again. After that time, he began to search ahead of where I was calling, but he was always looking around attempting to locate coyotes coming to the calling sounds. He spotted a coyote coming to the call one day before I did, and he went bawling after it, and chased it away. I did not want to reprimand him, but I teased him, and told him he had been dumb, as he was supposed to bring the coyote back. I know full well he did not understand what I was saying, but he full well understood the teasing tone of voice and he did not like to be teased about anything.

The next coyotes that I called in were old aggressive coyotes, and when he went to chase them, they only ran a short distance and turned to square away with him. He stood his ground, and bawled continually, looking back over his shoulder towards where I was sitting. There was too much wide open grassland between us for me to attempt to sneak close enough for a shot, so I just sat silently and waited to see what would transpire.

It was a hot summer morning and getting hotter as the sun climbed higher in the sky. George got hot and thirsty, so his nose led him to a nearby water reservoir. He drank, and then chased the coyotes away as they attempted to get a drink. He was always very jealous and did not like to share anything. After filling up with water, he began to worry about where I was, so he started to slowly trudge back towards where he had last saw me, stopping anytime one of the coyotes would get too close to him. Eventually he led the coyotes back to me, and I shot the large male coyote.

When George had been real small, I took him with me into a large prairie dog town, and let him watch me shoot them with a .22 caliber rifle. I wanted him to not fear the crack of a rifle shot. After he saw one get hit, he got so excited he almost jumped out the window over my shoulders, so I let him out to run to the dead prairie dog. Later, I took him to the prairie dog town and shot them with the big rifle. He soon learned to not be afraid of a gunshot, and also what the kerplop sound of a bullet striking flesh meant. So he knew what had happened, and he ran to the big male coyote and started to maul him, and shake him. The female coyote ran away, and then stopped about three hundred yards. She was watching the dog and her male partner. So I squeaked a hurt squeal on the open reed call. She came running back. Poor George was so involved in what he was doing he did not see her coming. She ran up behind him and grabbed him by the tail. He yiked, spun around and started to chase her. Since they were both hot and tired, he did not chase her too far, and then he turned around and came back to the male coyote. He sat down, guarding the carcass. She run up to about twenty feet and stopped. I shot her too.

After that day, I am not too sure which of us was having the most fun hunting coyotes, as George seemed to live for it all.

Then one day Ward Witte came to visit, and we went to an area to search for some coyotes to call and shoot. George brought two coyotes out of the timber and Ward shot one the first day. It was a bit comical, as when the dog and coyotes were coming back, they got down wind of where I had parked the pickup. The coyote kept

George and a coyote in a trap when he was about five months old.

trying to lead George back to the pickup. Ward could not get a good shot the first two times without hitting the pickup.

George did not like having Ward with us, as he did not like sharing his seat on that side of the pickup, and Ward teased him a bit which did not help with his jealous nature. The next day, I let George out of the pickup to look for coyote sign while we rode slowly behind on a four wheel trail in some tall timber country. I am quite positive it was his jealous nature that caused the mishap, as well as the fact that Ward and I were talking as we slowly drove along that caused the accident to happen.

Somehow George had gotten behind us, and then ran up alongside the pickup on the passenger side to rush right in front of the pickup to inspect a fresh coyote dropping. He knew better than to get in front of the pickup that close, but I am positive it was his jealous nature wanting to get to the dropping before Ward did. I could not see him from the driver side, and Ward was looking at me as we were talking, and I ran over the dog. The sickening clunk and the screaming wail of the dog will be in my memory forever.

We both feared the worst and Ward grabbed his pistol as we got out of the pickup. At first it looked very bad, as George seemed not to be able to get up, but he soon managed to start pulling himself with his front legs, and managed to get one hind leg working. He went to the passenger side of the pickup, and managed to get one front foot into the open door, as he attempted to get into the cab. So we gently loaded him and rushed back to town and the local veterinarian.

George and the veterinarian knew each other very well. George had gotten so many porcupine quills in his face when he was small that the vet had to remove as many as possible and treat him with antibiotics for the ones impossible to remove. Another time, George thought he was a dachshund again and had crawled into a coyote den, but the female coyote was in there and had torn a large piece of hide loose before he could get out, and the vet had to sew him back together. Later, he had chewed up and swallowed a hard ball baseball, which the vet had to operate to remove from his clogged up intestines. I know it was his jealousy that had gotten him into that pickle too, as he was always jealous of the youngest boy and his friends when they played catch with that ball. He had been a steady customer at the rural veterinarian shop.

When the vet examined him, he said he had a cracked pelvis, but seemed to be all right otherwise. Luckily nothing internal seemed to be too damaged. He set the pelvis as best he could, then wrapped his pelvis area with the only elastic bandage that he had large enough for the job. It was a hot pink color.

George looked a pathetic site later when we carried him into my home with his hot pink diaper on. I lay him on the floor, and told the wife that he needed to be kept out of bright light for a couple more hours until he came completely out of the anesthesia. Ward and I went back to where I needed to work. When we came home much later, the women had George stretched out completely on our waterbed. Darn dog!

George healed up quite well, but it slowed him down quite a bit, plus he would tire out sooner. All of which only improved his performances as a coyote calling dog.

For a period of time, I called and shot more coyotes with George than the airplane was even killing. Many times I would have calls from several ranchers losing lambs to coyotes, so I would not be able to get to a place for several days. When I would explain that to the ranchers, I would get a reply, something like, "Well, ok, if you can't make it, could you please send the dog?"

Craig O'Gorman was working in the county adjacent to where I was working. One day he called and asked if I would have time to bring my dog over and help him with some coyotes he was having serious problems with.

Before I tell that story, let me go back again to the days when George Good, Craig, and I would have discussions about killing problem coyotes. Both George and Craig would usually belittle calling coyotes, saying they could trap more coyotes than was possible to call and shoot, and they didn't have the time to waste attempting to call coyotes. Both men had called and shot coyotes, as well as worked with one of the best coyote callers in the state ADC program. So for Craig to call and even ask had to take a bit of effort on his part.

As we were driving into the area where Craig had been struggling with the killer coyotes, we saw a fresh killed lamb. We examined it, and started to look for tracks, and I let George out of the pickup. He made a half circle, hit fresh coyote odor, bawled and headed straight into some timber. Craig and I both grabbed our guns and started to follow, but before we made it into the timber, George came back out of the trees with a coyote following him. I shot the coyote, and George did his chew on them routine while Craig and I walked to where it lay. While we were standing there discussing everything, George went back into the trees and was soon barking hard and another coyote started to howl. Craig and I both followed along into the tall timber area.

In a few minutes George again came back towards us with a second coyote following along in hot pursuit. Craig and I had split apart several yards, and George saw Craig, so he led the coyote to him. Since Craig did not know exactly what to expect while working with the dog, he took a little longer shot than necessary and missed the coyote. When the coyote turned and ran, George followed it, and soon they were returning again. Craig shot again, only to have the coyote run back into the thicker timber area. George went and sat down. Craig kept trying to encourage him to go after the coyote, but

George just ignored him, by walking away, then sitting down again. It was mid morning by that time, and the sun had gotten hot. George just acted like he was hot and was not going to hunt any more.

When I snuck over to where they were, George came to greet me, and then he turned and started to walk in the direction the coyote had gone. He was soon barking excitedly again, but the coyote would not follow him back to where we were, so we snuck into the thicker timber and I saw the coyote sitting down. I shot it where it was sitting. When we examined it, we saw where Craig had hit the animal, low and way far back.

To be fair about this story, Craig had fallen earlier and hit his gun on something that had knocked the scope sight off.

We both had a good chuckle about George not going to work that hard if Craig could not shoot well enough to hit a coyote. George had more than a bit of character about him.

Over several years, I called and shot coyotes with George in Montana, North and South Dakota, Colorado, New Mexico, and Texas. But as he started to grow older, he began to slow down with pains as arthritis began to develop in his injured hips. As he got worse, I bought a male Blue Lacey pup.

There are many stories possible to relate about the trials and tribulations of those two while the pup, that I had named Joe, was growing up with Jealous George. However let me give you some idea, by telling one regular routine that developed. I had built an insulated dog house in the back yard, which was plenty large enough for them both, but George would not allow Joe into the dog house, so I cut another door in the back and built a divider panel in the middle of the dog house. George would sleep in one side for two days in a row while Joe slept in the other side, then George would take over the side that Joe had been in. As long as George was alive, the two of them went through this regular two day swap sides of the dog house routine.

The young dog was super smart, and it did not take too long for George to teach him what he needed to do while coyote hunting. They would race to get to a fresh coyote dropping first, or where a coyote had urinated. While calling, Joe had the advantage of youth and speed when they charged to meet approaching coyotes, but it

George and Joe competing with each other barking at a trapped coyote.

took him several tries to realize he was suppose to bring the coyotes back, and not just chase them. The problem was that he would come back to where old George was standing and barking, and not lead them back to me. The two dogs would then make a stand where they were, barking and howling at the coyotes. I could normally sneak close enough to shoot the coyotes, but I wanted the young dog to realize he needed to lead the coyotes back to where I was. So I had to take only him with me and leave old George home. When we returned, George would meet us, and howl and bark at me, chewing me out for leaving him at home, and then he would charge at Joe growling.

One very cold late winter day, I let both dogs out to do their duty and make the rounds. The young dog soon came back to the door of the house wanting inside, which was not too unusual, as he did not have enough hair for the harsh cold windy days in Montana. I just figured old George was making his usual tour, as he had quite a distance he would travel every morning. He was thirteen years old, and had established a routine that he followed every day. He had several old widow ladies that would feed or pamper him along his travel routes at the edge of town.

Some time later, a neighbor came to the door and told me he

thought George had been hit on the road, as he was lying funny in the driveway. He was unconscious and shivering. I loaded him into the pickup and rushed to veterinarian again. The vet said he had a very bad stroke. He told me he may be able to save him, but doubted if he would be able to walk correctly ever again. I told him "No, I wouldn't want anyone to do that to me, so I am not going to do that to that old dog, just put him to sleep."

As I mentioned Joe did not have enough hair for the super cold below zero days in Montana, so I made him a fur coyote coat. When I put it on him the first few times, he would hang his head, acting totally embarrassed. He knew what the coyote fur was, no doubt, even though it was tanned fur with no coyote odor, yet the very first time I put it on him in the house, he acted afraid, like maybe I may be going to shoot him, or something. I can't say that he ever got to where he liked to wear the coyote coat, but he did learn that when I put it on him, we were usually going to the hills hunting. If we had to stay home for two or three days waiting for the blowing snow to subside, he would go get his coat and drag it to me, wanting to go as soon as the storm would be over.

Joe eventually turned into the very best possible coyote calling dog that I have ever heard about or saw. I one time managed to kill five coyotes in some tall timber country that he would keep lead-

Joe with his coyote coat on.

Joe barking at a coyote in a trap.

ing back to me, each time I would shoot one of the others.

I called and shot coyotes with Joe in Montana, North and South Dakota, Wyoming, Nebraska, Colorado, Idaho, Texas, and California.

While in California, I shot a bobcat that came to the call, and when Joe ran to it, it was not dead. The two of them locked jaws, and the bobcat's eye tooth poked a hole through the top of the dog's nose.

While not as steady a customer for the veterinarians as old George had been, he did pay many visits to vets across the country getting repairs. He even got bit on his face by a rattlesnake.

Probably the worst damage was done while calling coyotes out of Livingston, Montana. A friend who was quite a bow hunter wanted a chance to shoot a coyote with his bow. To make a long story short, he did shoot a coyote with an arrow but it was not dead and when Joe chased it into some heavy brush, somehow the coyote managed to tear a large piece of hide from Joe's side.

The problem with pets is that they become family in time, but they just do not live as long. Joe lived longer than George had, but at sixteen, he too passed away.

I would be derelict while relating trapping stories if I did not include a few stories about the many characters that I met over the many years and places I have been.

Perhaps one of the most colorful individuals would be Sherrill Farwell. I met Sherrill shortly after I had moved to Ekalaka, Montana, to do predator control work in Carter County.

Man oh man, where to start to begin to describe the old rascal? In time, I would learn that he had been born and raised in the home where I first met him, on a homestead between Ekalaka, and Alzada, Montana. His father had been a sheep rancher as had Sherrill for most of his life.

For several years, Sherrill had owned a small tavern in Alzada, Montana, several miles south of the old home ranch. Sherrill was very proud of the fact that he was what he termed a card mechanic, which essentially meant that he could deal from anywhere in a deck of cards without getting caught. He had been a card and dice gambler for most of his life while operating a sheep ranch and the tavern in Alzada. I very seriously now regret not having taken a tape recorder with me to his home to listen to his many stories. What a colorful dangerous life the man had lived!

The quaint village of Alzada, Montana is located in the far south eastern corner of Montana, which situates it close to near where North and South Dakota, as well as Wyoming all border next to Montana. In the days when the law could not cross state borders to make an arrest, the town became a home to many crooks that would travel into bordering states to steal for a living. Sherrill told me many different stories about people that lived there through those times, and of course being a gambler, Sherrill himself was often one of those making trips into bordering states.

Sherrill was in his early 70's when I first met him. He had no teeth, little hair, but what gray hair he did have he wore long and rather straggly most of the time. When he talked, he would kind of sputter through his toothless lips, often actually scattering bits of spray from his mouth when he would get excited. He was not a very tall man, but still very active when he wanted to be, and walked with a short quick stride, or short quick steps tittering a bit if any actual work became involved when anyone was around.

He was a con man with almost everything he did, and always had someone around to do any physical labors that needed to be done, even though I would learn in time the old rascal was much spryer than he wanted anyone to know if he was doing something he wanted to do. Sherrill was always wheeling and dealing on something; often trading for machinery, vehicles, or just groceries, food, or some form of booze. He was a very likeable devil in many ways, and would do anything he could to help his friends or family, and he of course treated most people like they really were his friends. He loved the game of baseball.

Carter County, Montana, had more sheep than any other county in Montana, and a great deal of that had to be attributed to much of the southern part of the county consisting of hard clay soil with little annual rainfall, growing mostly low scrubby sagebrush, and very little water, as well as a very efficient aerial predator control program and a pilot by the name of Alvin Tatge who lived in Alzada, Montana.

Sherrill told me the story about how Alvin Tatge was on his way to Alaska to look for a job hunting for wolves, when he developed airplane problems. Alvin had been a pilot during the Second World War, and since his discharge from the military, he had flown a spray plane for awhile, but did not like that work, so decided he would go to Alaska. He landed his airplane on the highway, just outside of Alzada and walked to town. He went into the bar that Sherrill owned, looking for a telephone. One thing led to another, while they visited, and since there was no motel or hotel in town at that time, Sherrill offered him a shed that he owned behind the bar to stay in while he waited for parts for his airplane to be freighted in. From that point, the story got long, but the short version is that they became good friends in the time it took for the airplane parts to arrive, and when they did arrive, he and Sherrill went coyote hunting from the airplane for a couple of the local sheep ranchers that were friends of Sherrill's.

Alvin Tatge never left Alzada after that, because the local sheep ranchers eventually put together a program to keep him there

Clara on the left and Sherrill on the right during their 50th Wedding Anniversary standing behind a picture of them right after they were married.

Sherrill Farwell holding a coyote killed in his sheep pasture.

to hunt coyotes. In time the county hired Alvin and he eventually was taking care of all the sheep herds in the county. He is a very skilled airplane pilot, capable of flying a cub airplane better than probably anyone anywhere, and almost as good a shotgun marksman as well.

Carter County did not have a coyote trapper to do predator control work for all the years that Alvin Tatge had been there. There was a bit of concern with many of the old time sheep ranchers, that I was there attempting to replace Alvin Tatge.

The first day I drove into Sherrill Farwell's yard, he and his wife Clara were busy in front of the house. Clara was mowing the lawn, and Sherrill was picking up limbs that had fallen from the many trees in the yard. They both came to greet me as I stepped out of the pickup.

When I introduced myself to them, Sherrill said, "Oh, so you're that trapper guy I been hearing about, eh?" "I heard there was some new hot shot around."

When I chuckled at Sherrill, and told him that I was no hot shot, just a coyote trapper, looking for a place to trap coyotes, Sherrill got very excited. He said, "I don't want no damn coyote traps put on my land! I don't want any three legged coyotes running around that Alvin Tatge will have to hunt for!"

Clara, cut Sherrill off, and said, "Why don't you come in the house and visit, I have a fresh pot of coffee on, and a pie baking in the oven that should be almost done."

Clara would prove out to be as much of an individual character as old Sherrill was. The two of them had been married for many years, and what one was, the other was not. Clara was always a perfect lady, dressed well, and with makeup on even while doing hard dirty chores.

I thanked her for the offer, and started to make some kind of excuse, but Clara wouldn't take no for an answer as she turned to Sherrill and said, "Come Daddy, come in the house, you guys can visit in there."

Sherrill was a bit reluctant at first, but as Clara pushed and kept insisting, we both finally followed her into the house, listening to her apologize and explain that the perfectly kept household was such a mess.

While inside drinking coffee, I managed to explain that I did not want to compete with Alvin Tatge, but was really wanting to work with him, and that it was in fact Alvin that had suggested I go meet up with Sherrill.

Alvin had seen a coyote in a thick tall pine tree timber cluster, near to where Sherrill's sheep were, but had been unable to get a shot at it in the tall trees. He thought perhaps I may be able to get it, since he was concerned that it would begin to kill Sherrill's sheep at night. When I explained all that to Sherrill, he immediately warmed up towards me, but was very cautious as he asked question after question.

What started out as a difficult meeting, would in time turn into a very close friendship to the point that many years later their two boys would beg me into doing the eulogy for Clara's funeral, a few years after Sherrill had died.

Sherrill hated coyotes with a passion, having struggled with them killing sheep since he was a young boy. A couple of stories I think are worth telling about him to illustrate this point.

From starting out by not wanting any traps of any kind on his property, Sherrill would soon call me if he saw a coyote track or heard one howl. He would go with me while I set the traps or snares, then he would check them for me.

One morning after a fresh snow storm, Sherrill called quite excited, saying he had found coyote tracks right behind his house. I told him I could not come right away, but would meet him there in the afternoon. When I went there, I followed the coyote tracks and Sherrill followed beside in my pickup. I located a place where the coyote had chased a jack rabbit through some thick low scrub brush to a hole in the ground where the rabbit had gone. I told Sherrill that I thought I could catch the coyote in a snare in that brush, because I was sure it would return to look for that jack rabbit. I set the snare with Sherrill watching closely, because he was worried about having a snare on his land that may catch a sheep.

The next morning I went there again, and Sherrill and I were going to go around the sheep pasture and look for coyote tracks, but on the way we went to where I had set the snare the evening before.

We saw the coyote struggling from quite a distance, and Sherrill was very excited, worried that it may get away. When we got close, I took out my pistol, and Sherrill reached for it, saying "let me shoot that dirty no good #$&* thing, trying to eat my sheep will he." I chuckled and let him have the pistol.

I am not sure exactly what Sherrill was expecting, but I believe he thought it would be like a coyote in a trap, and not be able to move around too much. The snare was ten feel long, which meant it could run around in a twenty foot circle. It was standing clear to the far end of the snare when Sherrill started to approach, but when he got close it started to run around, wrapping the snare cable around Sherrill's legs, tripping him. It would be impossible to describe the yelling and cussing that followed, as old Sherrill struggled to get up in the brush and the scared coyote attempting to escape, tripped Sherrill a second time.

Sherrill had dropped the gun, and finally came scooting from the brush patch, cussing a blue streak while I was holding my sides laughing hard.

Another time, a neighbor called Sherrill to tell him that he had saw two coyotes in a pasture near Sherrill's place.

We went into the neighbor's pasture, and I let my dog George out of the pickup. It wasn't long before he started bawling on trail, so I hurried Sherrill out of the pickup and over the side of the hill and told him to hide. It wasn't very long before George came back up the hill with one coyote in hot pursuit. George saw Sherrill, and started his direction. Sherrill curled up into a ball, while George led the coyote in front of Sherrill at a distance of like ten feet. The coyote stopped there, looking at Sherrill sensing something amiss, and I shot it.

To hear Sherrill tell the story for a couple years after that, he said that he had gotten blood splattered on him when I shot the coyote, which was not true, but I am not too sure that in Sherrill's mind he believed it might have happened. Another time, a coyote hung up and would not come any closer, and I shot it at about four hundred yards. Sherrill would tell the story that it was so far away he could hardly see it, and had tired out before he could walk to where it was laying. He loved to embellish on a story if the opportunity presented itself.

Sherrill's ranch bordered beside the Forest Service boundary on the back side. I managed to get a coyote to howl at me from high on the hillside, just inside the forest, and with George's help, I managed to call a large male coyote and kill it. George followed the female back to the den, and the female crawled into the den and kept George bawling in front of the hole. I plugged the den, then went to my pickup and got some traps. I carried the traps to the den and set three traps in two different entranceways.

When I took the male coyote to Sherrill's place to show him, and told him about the den, he wanted to go with me the next day when I checked the traps. It was a quite long steep climb up a long narrow ridge to get where the den was. But Sherrill insisted he wanted to go.

The next morning, I had the old female in one trap, and one large pup coyote that was not much larger than a large house cat in another trap. I killed the female, then captured the pup, and tied its legs together and its mouth shut. I was going to take it home to put into a cage to catch urine from, but Sherrill started objecting right away, saying, "By gosh you better have a good pen, as that thing will grow up and come back here and eat my sheep." I assured him I did have a good strong pen, but could tell by the scowl on his face and grumbling under his breath that he still did not approve.

Since I was going to drag the female coyote out, Sherrill snatched the pup coyote from my hands, saying he could carry the pup back to the pickup. I don't think we had taken twenty steps when Sherrill stumbled and fell on the coyote with both knees, then another twenty feet; he stumbled again and slammed the coyote against a tall pine tree. All the way back down the hill, he kept stumbling and falling, although he had gone up the steep hill with little trouble at all. By the time we reached the pickup, the coyote pup was little more than a limp bundle of fur. Sherrill asked me where I wanted to put it, and I told him I did not want the darn thing, to just throw it in the ditch. He sputtered and stammered with a shocked look on his face saying, "I thought you were going to raise it?"

I said, "You dang old scoundrel you know full well you killed it when you jumped on it with both your knees at the top of the hill, and you made damn sure all the rest of the way down the hill!"

Sherrill got a sheepish look on his face and sputtered, "Yeah, yeah, well maybe, but it was all accidents." I just laughed at him!

As gruff as Sherrill liked to pretend that he was, he had a big soft spot about several things, and was very superstitious. He liked to act tough, but was actually quite scared of many things.

One far corner of his sheep pasture, Sherrill told me a rattlesnake lived there that had been trying to bite him for several years. He said every time he got off a horse or out of his pickup anywhere near there, the darn snake would attempt to bite him. Walking through the area alone one day in the early fall, I found a rattlesnake den with several rattlesnakes laying around the opening. I destroyed the den, and nobody ever saw another rattlesnake near that area again.

One late spring day, Sherrill and I were checking a few coyote traps on one of his adjoining neighbor's ranch. There was a young female red fox in a trap that obviously had just recently had pups. Sherrill said, "Just release her, she won't bother anything around here, and she is too far away from my sheep to bother me." He had a soft spot about baby animals of any kind.

I managed to grab the fox by the tail, and then grabbed her with my other hand by the back of her neck. Releasing the hold on her tail, I used that hand to push down one side of the trap springs, and stepped on the other spring lever. When the jaws opened, I picked her up and carried her to the pickup, where Sherrill was sitting watching with the door open. He started sputtering that some day I was going to get bitten handling animals like that. I started laughing, and the devil made me throw the fox into his lap.

The frightened little fox, landed on his lap, and instantly sprang out of the open door, while Sherrill started cussing, yelling, and almost flew to the opposite side of the pickup seat, with his arms wrapped around his head.

Almost a year later, I grabbed a badger by the loose skin of its back, and removed the trap while Sherrill watched, but as quick as I took a step towards the pickup, Sherrill slammed the door shut, and pushed down the lock. Sputtering and cussing loudly all the while he was attempting to get the pickup secure.

I could tell many stories about Sherrill and Clara, but let me attempt to relate a story that Sherrill told me about Alvin Tatge, the airplane pilot. He said that since there were no motels or hotels in Alzada, Sherrill had told Alvin that he could stay in a building that was behind the bar. He said they had fixed it up and made it livable, putting a table, chairs, and bed in the building, but it did not have a heater. They found an old wood stove and hauled it into the shed, with pipe to vent the smoke through the roof. The old stove sat in the same place all summer long, and each time that Sherrill asked Alvin how come he had not put the pipe up, Alvin always told him he did not have any way to cut a hole in the roof, but he would get it done soon. The first cold snap hit early in September, and Sherrill went to check on Alvin in the morning, and saw that the pipe was sticking from the roof and smoke was coming out of it. When he asked Alvin how he gotten that done so fast, he said Alvin just got a sheepish look on his face. Sherrill thought for a moment and said you shot a hole through the roof with your shotgun didn't you, to which Alvin sheepishly smirked and nodded his head in the affirmative.

One day while everyone was working sheep, Alvin landed his airplane in front of the house. Someone made comment that he had landed it in a very short distance. Alvin said that it was easy to do when the wind was blowing. There were a couple questions, and Alvin said he could land it in the corral if the wind was blowing hard enough. One of the local ranchers said, "Well, you're pretty good but that corral is awful small."

The next day while the ranchers were finishing working with Sherrill's sheep, Alvin flew over them, banked the airplane around, into the wind, and set the plane down in the corral. They had to take one side of the corral down, however so he could get the plane back out of the corral. Sherrill grumbled, complained, and cussed about that incident for years, telling the story over and over again.

When I first learned that I would be moving to Ekalaka, Montana, I realized that I had no idea even where it was. I had never been there before. Talking with Craig O'Gorman on the telephone, he told me to come to his home, first, and he would take me there, as he had a dead horse he needed to pick up, and he would introduce me to some people I needed to know if I was going to be living there.

The Walters family are great people, but anything except a normal family. Each is an individual that would again have to be characterized simply as unique individuals: both Vernon and Bernice, as well as each one of their children.

When you enter into the Walters home, you enter beside a large picture window that is one end of the kitchen, which Bernice is guaranteed to begin apologizing about. It is always clean and organized, but not in Bernice's mind. The kitchen is separated from the rest of the home with a bar room counter, that has comfortable tall stools. Bernice will begin fussing in the kitchen, usually putting a kettle of water on the fire, for coffee, and Vernon will set on a tall stool at the far end of the bar counter, as they suggest you sit down and have a cup of coffee, or a drink: a drink, meaning beer or whiskey. It is just normal for a guest to sit at the counter.

Craig O'Gorman stayed at their home several years earlier while he was trapping with a partner. When he took me there, the yard had a fence in front of the house to keep livestock off what little grass and few flowering plants were there, but the pigs, sheep, cattle and horses roamed freely beside the house, and between all the out buildings situated near by.

Vernon Walters had a large chew of tobacco in his cheek, and wore western cowboy clothing with low heel cowboy boots. He had put the dead horse on a flatbed trailer situated in the driveway behind the house. I am positive he brags to this day about having sold a dead horse. Vernon is always working an angle of some sort.

Local people call Vernon simply "Pappy," because he has a way with children, and tucks them under his wing, buddying up with them, with a joking mannerism. Everyone calls Bernice, "Mother Bernice," because she will do anything for anyone to help them, yet she is a bit bossy with a gruff mannerism that she is proud of, but it doesn't take a visitor very long to realize that it is all a false front show as her tender side comes out. However, with that said, I am sure that her hard side would be difficult to deal with if someone ever crossed her.

Eastern Montana is a vast land of rolling sagebrush and/or farm land with extreme weather. Hot and very dry in the summer

The Walters Family

months, cold and deep snow that blows around with steady cold winds in the winter. Ranch homes are several miles apart since farms and ranches are large, because it takes a good deal of acreage in the arid region to produce enough to support a family. All the towns are small and several miles apart. High school athletics are very important, as it supplies one of the few forms of recreation for people to gather together. Basketball is quite important, since it continues through the long cold winters, and attending basketball games on the weekends provides an excuse to go to town and visit with friends.

Vernon Walters had been a local high school basketball star, so it would only follow that the two twin red headed Walters girls would be basketball players. The girls were just starting high school when I moved to Ekalaka, and when they found out that I had played college basketball, they soon drug me outside to play basketball on the driveway where a basket and backboard was planted into the hard soil. I had never played basketball with girls, and will admit quickly that I was very impressed by how rough they played, which made things a bit awkward for me, not knowing how hard I dared to play back. I showed them a couple of moves to make, and some defensive strategy, since they were determined to make the town basketball team. For the next four years I dared not miss a girls basketball game, and if something came up that mandated that I must miss a game, the girls would call me on the telephone and go over things play by play, asking what they could have done differently. With time, I have grown very close to the Walters family and think of them as family.

South and east of the Walters ranch, I would face my first serious coyote challenge in Carter County. There is a ranch, which at that time was owned by two extravagant older brothers that were having very serious coyote killing going on, nightly. It had been taking place for a couple years, but had just recently gotten consistently serious and regular. The men were taking turns, sleeping with the sheep on the bed ground.

The area is rough bentonite soil with serious eroded away creeks, higher red colored scorio gravel covered hills, bordered by timber and thick juniper cedar shrubs. The coyote had killed in virtually every nook and cranny of the large pasture. Because the pasture was the roughest terrain anywhere near the area, it seemed apparent that it was residing within the same pasture as the sheep. It seemed even more likely, since Alvin Tatge had flown the area several times, attempting to find the coyote from the airplane, because the thick cedars and tall timber would provide cover difficult to locate a coyote in from the air.

I spent a week setting traps just outside of the sheep pasture, and put a few snares in the fence lines, plus I did a lot of walking, searching for tracks in the ragged creek bottoms.

From the location where I found many of the dead sheep, it started to become obvious that the coyote was doing most of the killing in the daylight hours.

I got out of bed way before daylight and parked my pickup on a high hill, across the deepest part of the canyon from where the sheep were bedding down. As daylight slowly arrived, I could see the sheep still bedded, and a pickup parked with them where one of the men was sleeping. I glassed the entire area closely with my binoculars.

When the sun climbed higher, and the sheep began to stir and get up to graze, I saw that the pickup headed back to the closest living quarters. A few minutes later, I spotted the coyote crossing the deep canyon to the east of where I was sitting. He was heading towards the sheep. I grabbed my rifle and slid out of my truck, and got into the bottom of a deep washed side drainage, then ran to the mouth of the small drainage. I had the wind in my favor, as I lay down watching the sheep trickle down from the opposite side of the main creek. I saw the coyote cross the top of two small humps of the jumbled area, as it was heading directly towards the sheep. I picked the top of a small ridgeline, where I anticipated it would stop when it came into view of the sheep, and waited, looking through the scope waiting for the coyote to reach that spot.

The coyote already had quite a reputation, as people had attempted to trap for it all winter long, the airplane had searched for it in the winter, and several people had went into the area with snowmobiles in the winter to attempt to run it down and kill it. People had searched and hunted for it from saddle horses, in the spring,

Coyote with early serious stage of mange.

Poor old coyote with one leg shot off high in late stages of serious mange.

with others situated at strategic locations with rifles around where the saddle horse riders were riding through the roughest terrains while the airplane flew over head. Few had gotten a glimpse of the coyote.

Through the scope, I watched patiently, as the coyote walked up the side of the ridgeline. I just felt sure it would stop when it reached the crest of the ridge. Everything was working exactly as I had anticipated that it would, until it got to the exact place where I figured on getting a good standing shot. It hesitated briefly there, then spun around to look behind, and quickly started running, like it had just been shot at. It continued to run, past some of the lead sheep, and was heading towards some tall timber to my right. I followed its progress with my cross hairs on it through the scope. I am not a good running shot. However I had been following it in the scope long enough to have its gait down, and when I shot, it just dropped and disappeared from my view in the taller sagebrush.

I have no idea what made the coyote begin to run when it hit the exact place where I had anticipated getting at shot it earlier, but over the years I have learned that coyotes have a sixth sense of sudden imminent danger. That is the best explanation I can offer, but I believe all wildlife have a bit of this same sense of danger at times. The coyote turned out to be an old male coyote, with a very short stubby tail, and one hind leg that had been broken at some time that healed slightly crooked. It was missing one eye, and one ear was shredded and hung down. It had been through something very serious at some time or other.

Killing that particular coyote was a good start for my predator control operations in Carter County.

It just occurred to me that someone reading this may begin to think that I hate coyotes. Let me quickly say that I dislike many of the things coyotes do; killing more than they eat, killing savagely, crippling many animals that they do not get killed, killing competition like foxes that live in the same area, or killing just to be killing. However, with that said, over the many years of studying the animals, I have gained much respect for the coyote's intelligence, and will to survive. I often have more respect for coyotes in general than I do for humans, as it crosses my mind often that I doubt if the human race could survive with the daily difficulties that coyotes face. Most coyote adults will lay down their life to protect their young. I sometimes find myself pitying some individual coyote; I have seen one live for two years with a broken back in a prairie dog town, another that survived with his lower jaw shot off but survived by eating warm cow manure, and at least four or five individuals that have had one leg shot off just below the shoulder, and while skinning coyotes I often find old broken bones that have healed, but the worst possible slow death that any animal can suffer is Sarcoptic Mange! Mange is a tiny mite that burrows down into the skin and eats away the roots of the hair follicles. The constant itch produced by the tiny Mange mites cause the suffering animals to scratch, roll, and rub until large sores develop. The sores eventually develop infection that will kill the infected animal. Luckier ones may freeze because of a lack of hair to survive extreme cold. Yet, it is impossible not to feel for the animals suffering without any technique to cure themselves.

❖　❖　❖

I suspect that it is just human nature to always think, like sheep or cattle do, that the grass is always a little greener on the other side of the fence. My first out-of-state trapping venture was a partner venture with Craig O'Gorman. We went to the Red Desert, in Wyoming, and put snares in the tall sagebrush pockets for coyotes.

One experience stands out in my mind while we were in the Red Desert. We had been seeing a good deal of badger activity while there, but had been concentrating our efforts for coyotes only. Then one day we saw a very fresh dug hole, with fresh dirt on top of the snow. Craig asked if I thought we could snare it. I set a snare at the entrance to the hole, and the next day a badger was caught, but went into the hole. The snare was a ten foot long coyote snare, and it went all the way the length of the snare. We attempted to dig it out, but the frozen ground made digging next to impossible, so thinking that the snare cable had a breaking strength of over 1000 pounds, we figured we could pull the badger from the hole by hooking the snare to the ball on Craig's pickup. Was a reasonable sounding idea, but the cable broke before we could pull the badger from that hole. I had heard as a young teenager that it was impossible to pull a badger out of a hole, and that experience just proved it.

Maybe the reason I remember it so well, is because while we were struggling around, I stepped into a depression covered with snow, tripped and fell, and sprained my ankle, quite severely.

A couple years later, I was contacted by the Maine Department of Fish and Wildlife. They asked if I could come to Maine to work with their game wardens, and show them how to snare coyotes in deer yards during the winter. My initial reaction wanted to say "NO!" However the more I listened to him talk, I began to think, so I figured, "Why not? An expense paid trip to go see Maine would be interesting."

I enjoyed that trip to Maine, even though the temperatures were well below zero all the time that I was there. I had to chuckle a couple times, as they worried about me freezing my cheek bones, since they were unaware that their temperatures were actually much nicer than what I had just come from in Montana.

The highlight of the trip was the wonderful, nice people that I met while I was there. One ol rascal in particular, a man by the name of Harold Blanchard, was affectionately known simply as "Doc."

Doc Blanchard was a biologist at that time, in charge of a large area. He had the respect of his superiors as well as all those that worked under him. Colorful would be a very good description to describe Doc's personality. His New England accent of pronouncing "R" as "urr," simply accentuated his personality. I took an instant like to him, and we are very good friends to this day. He is now in his 80's. While I was there, Doc made a statement that I still quote often today: "The most dangerous animal in the woods is a young biologist whose ink is not quite dry on his degree."

While I was in Maine, I attempted to help them understand that game wardens would not have the time to be able to protect the deer yards as they had hoped. It took a couple of years for them to fully understand that I had been correct that the game wardens could not keep up and do their regular job as well. They again called me on the phone and asked if I would mind coming back to Maine and assist with some training to some special selected trappers. So I made a second trip to Maine, in much more pleasant early fall weather.

What I was not aware of before arriving in Maine for the second time was that I was walking into a political hotbed. Sportsmen were upset about deer being killed, livestock owners were upset about livestock being killed, and there had been a couple of coyotes and people encounters. One in particular that I remember was a man who went into a manhole to do some sort of repairs or other, and coyotes kept him penned in the manhole until help arrived.

We traveled to several cities, and put on brief town hall type meetings with biologists, and game wardens, talking about coyotes and the problems, and myself discussing a few possible options. At each meeting, the talks were basically the same. The biologist gave some statistics and in that segment he said that "X" number of coyotes would starve to death each winter in Maine's harsh winter climate, their first year. I tried to visit with him about that statement in private a couple times, but what did I know, being only a trapper from Montana. So finally the last meeting where there were state

Harold "Doc" Blanchard and antelope he shot in Montana.

Harold "Doc" Blanchard and his wife, Mercedes "Clay Basket."

representatives as well as most of the directors of the state Department of Natural Resources, I removed a one hundred dollar bill from my wallet and laid it on the podium, stating that if ANYONE could clinically prove to me that if even ONE coyote starved to death he could have that one hundred dollar bill. It caused quite a stir in the audience with lots of grumbles as well as chuckles.

It was almost a year and half later that I received a packet from the Maine State Department of Natural Resources, Fish and Wildlife Division. In the packet was a complete clinical report that was proof that a coyote had indeed starved to death. However, attached to the last page was an envelope with the word "Slim" written on it. Within the envelope was one final page of the clinical report, as well as my $100 with a note attached to it. The note said, "We thought we had you on this one, but it looks like this coyote over ate instead."

The last page of the report showed that the coyote had eaten a sole off a rubber overshoe and that it had lodged in the intestines, so that the animal could not digest any other food it may have eaten.

A couple of years later, Doc Blanchard came to Montana to go antelope hunting with me assisting. To give you a brief idea about Doc's colorful personality, I made him crawl on his hands and knees the last few yards to the top of a ridge, and then made him inch forward on his stomach to look over a herd of antelope. Later, he would swear in a gruff chuckle, that by golly he had to remove dry cow manure from his shirt pockets for two days. After seeing antelope up close for the first time, he would always refer to them as "pretty faces" from that time on, and of course with his New England accent of not pronouncing "R" correctly, it always came out as "puety faces."

When I was in Maine the first time, Doc showed me the beaver he had put up. I told him I didn't think I had ever seen better put up beaver, as they were thin as paper and the leather side of the hides were white as snow. He said his wife, referring to her as "Clay Basket" (in reference to the Indian lady in the TV series, "Lonesome Dove," that had just recently finished running for a few weeks on TV), had actually done most of the fleshing. While her real name is Mercedes, everyone still calls her "Clay Basket." I teased them that I was going to steal her and take her back to Montana with me, to which, she promptly agreed, and Doc would hug her quickly and say, "Oh no you don't! You are skinning my 'beaveus' woman." And even today, every phone conversation he will say to us both, "Oh no you don't, she is skinning my 'beaveus.'"

Somewhere over the years, I have lost being able to remember exact dates when things happened, but not too long after Doc came to Montana to hunt antelope, I received a phone call from Ed Courtney, who lived in El Paso, Texas at that time. Ed was working on using an endless tape recording to attract bobcats to his traps. The conversation went on for a long time, about sounds, volume, quiet time, and possible distance to the trap. It was a concept that made sense to me, yet, a concept that I envisioned problems with as well. I had been calling predators with a mouth call for several years, and the idea of an attraction sound near traps seemed a bit distracting from the trap. To again shorten a long story, Ed and I had several more phone conversations after that first one. Ed went on to have an electronic squeaker made instead of attempting to use a tape player. A year later, I found myself driving to El Paso to trap just north of there in New Mexico and test some of the squeakers with Ed.

Once again, as I sit here searching for words, I am struggling to attempt to describe Ed Courtney's personality and persona. Ed was a ranking officer in the western division of the U.S. Drug Enforcement Agency. Because he dealt often with life and death situations, Ed obviously has a very serious hard side to him. Yet he also has a child like innocent devilish, almost little girl like, giggly sense of humor as well. Nothing he likes better than to set someone up for a "gotcha" so he can giggle and tease.

Ed and I went coyote calling on the edge of El Paso. I did not have a license, so Ed had the only gun. I was doing most of the calling. Three coyotes came running hard towards the calling sounds. Ed was positioned to my right, on a little rise, and I was in a clump of greasewood. I was unsure if Ed had seen the coyotes, as they came right up the very bottom of the draw that I was laying in. I pulled my camouflage cap down over my face, and crowded as close to the ground as possible. The large male coyote came to a distance of about five feet in front of me, before he turned to leave. Ed shot him when he turned. Later he giggled and giggled when he kept saying he just wanted to see if the coyote would try to bite the cap off my head.

Several miles out of town, there was a large dairy milk operation, and it was not a bit unusual to see a coyote crossing the road to or from the dairy farm. One day I saw a coyote that had been hit by a vehicle, but it was not worth skinning, as when I saw it, it had been run over several times. Ed told me there were dead coyotes on that stretch of the road year-round. However, one night while returning from checking traps, there was a very fresh run over coyote lying on the busy freeway. I pulled over, ran back in the dark, dodging traffic, and quickly grabbed it, drug it to the pickup and threw it in the back.

Ed and I would meet every night, and go for supper, then go skin what each of us had caught during the day. I told Ed about the coyote I picked up on the road. He picked on me a bit about having

Ed Courtney making a bobcat set.

to find a freebee to have something to skin.

When we pulled up to where we did the skinning, Ed was there ahead of me, and threw his coyotes out of his pickup onto the ground, and was dragging them into the shed where we skinned. I got out of the pickup, and went to his pile of coyotes to help him drag them inside. While I was dragging in the last few coyotes, Ed went to my pickup to unload the coyotes I had. When I came back out of the shed, he was laughing his head off. The coyote that I had picked up on the road was actually a young light colored German Shepard dog and not a coyote at all. To this day, he will start his giggle and bring up my Montana Pale coyote that I picked up off the road in Texas.

After that first trip to the Desert Southwest, I made three more trips there. I love the desert, and find myself like a kid in Disney Land all the time while I am in the desert. There is always something else new to catch my eye and distract me. There is not a blade of grass the same as anywhere else I have been, much less the rest of the cactus or other vegetations. Yucca plants in Eastern Montana grow to about two feet tall if they are where good water is available, but in the desert the various types of yucca, that grow fifteen to twenty feet tall totally amaze me. The Spanish dagger plants that resemble even much larger yucca plants astounded me.

Even the animals like deer and coyotes are a bit different, and there are several other animals that I saw for the first time, such as the black tailed jack rabbits, little swift fox, javelina pigs, and ringtail cats. Several different kinds of birds, such as the famous road runners, and the different kinds of quail, would catch my attention. Even though it was winter time, and the nights would get bitter cold, the warm afternoons would find me studying some of the many different kinds of little lizards that would come out for the warm sunshine. I even killed three coon tail rattlesnakes, and one small sidewinder.

One quiet cool morning, I found myself on a long salient ridge line that overlooked some likely coyote country. I could not resist the temptation, so I grabbed my rifle along with mouth calls, and walked to where I had a good view. I sat with my back to some tall thick thorn brush, and began calling. I anticipated that coyotes

Me and my dog, George, standing beside Spanish dagger plant.

My youngest son, Bill, and his wife Cari, right after they graduated from Annapolis Naval Academy, standing in front of mounted lion rug.

would have been called in the area, so I attempted to sound like a fawn deer, rather than a rabbit. About the third time I called, I saw a pair of coyotes way below me, but just as I saw them, the brush behind me began to pop and snap. I at first figured it was probably some cattle, but then I heard grunts, and huffs. I forgot about the coyotes, and turned to defend myself from the unseen intruders. Several javelina pigs of three different sizes came rushing through the brush, scaring me, since I did not know what to expect from them. I stood up, quickly, and yelled. Pigs went every direction. It took several minutes to get my heart beat back to normal.

I found where a large mountain lion had walked down a small dry creek bottom where it had left a larger creek. I made a large dirt hole set, and used one of Ed's Squeaker units behind the hole, using a Sterling trap, hoping that it would be large and strong enough to hold a lion. The lion returned through the creek bottom a week later. It walked up to the dirt hole, and then went around the hole to the squeaker unit. Apparently much more interested in the noise than in anything else at the set.

I made another set up against a steep washed away bank of the creek, by making a very large dirt hole with half a coyote carcass in the hole. I also made barriers, and turned the set into a walk through set, and used rocks as stepping obstructions to guide the foot of any approaching animal to the trap. Three days later, I caught an ugly old male coyote that completely destroyed the set. I remade it again, hoping the lion would find the entire disturbance interesting enough to inspect.

The big lion never returned through that area while I was there. I had to return home to Montana to start my summer predator control operations in the early spring, and Ed asked me to leave the trap, and he would check it. Two days after I left, a young lion was in the trap. Ed killed it and skinned it for me. I later tanned the hide, and got a form, glass eyes, and mouth from Van Dykes taxidermist Supply Company, and made a rug with head and open mouth that I still have today.

That was the very first lion that I caught and over the years, since that time, I have caught several more much larger cats.

After my trips to Wyoming, Maine, New Mexico, and Texas,

I guess I became obsessed with wanting to see and trap in different parts of the United States.

I spent one winter trapping in Colorado with some friends. Bob Hanson was the man that talked me into coming to Colorado. Bob had retired a few years earlier from the Army. He had been a drill sergeant. He served the last few months of World War II, all of the Korean War, and most of the Vietnam War. Trapping and the outdoors was a form of mental therapy for Bob. He managed to survive his war time with only a couple of minor gunshot wounds, but after he retired from the military, he went to work on a barge on the Mississippi River, and crushed his right leg. The doctor wanted to amputate the leg, but Bob would not allow them to do that, and his right leg was fused together from his hip to his ankle; stiff and straight with no knee. Gruff, hard, and determined, he got around surprising well with his stiff leg. He refused to use a crutch or a cane.

Bob was affectionately known as Pierre, because he had been caught with a woman, in a compromising position (that I will leave up to your imagination to envision, rather than describe), during a late night drunken episode. I knew him as Pierre, and will refer to him from here on as Pierre.

Pierre had seen most of the worst things in war. He was unaware that he yelled loud and screamed all night long in his sleep. He drank Yukon Jack whiskey, straight from the bottle, from the time he got up in the morning. He would sip on the whiskey, lightly during the daytime, but when the day's work was through he would begin to drink heavily after supper was over each night, until he would stumble to bed to sleep in a drunken stupor.

Pierre's long military career had taught him how to get along well with most people. He was very smooth with the ladies and would usually have women eating out of his hand in a few minutes. Younger or older women, from little girls to old hardened gruff mountain grandmothers, they all liked Pierre. About the only people that he did not have any time for was people dressed up in a suit and tie, or someone attempting to put on airs of some sort or other that he saw through immediately. It was impossible not to like and respect Pierre once you got to know him.

Pierre was a very good coyote trapper, even though it was

Bob "Pierre" Hanson

difficult for him to get down with his stiff leg in many types of terrain, so he would have to pick and choose where he could make his sets. Setting snares was something he wanted to learn, and I think he would get a bit frustrated attempting to get around in the thicker tall sagebrush where I often set snares. So one day a fresh set of coyote tracks in the snow crossed the road, and went up a trail in some very open terrain. I told him to set a snare on that trail, but he looked at me and growled, saying you couldn't catch a coyote on a trail that was that open. So I laughed at him and said, "O.K. old man, you just sit your behind right there and watch how a real coyote trapper does things."

Two days later there was a coyote in the snare that I had set on that trail. Pierre, grumbled, and said, "That poor coyote must have been blind to stumble into that thing!"

We set traps for fox, coyotes, and bobcats, as well as beaver and mink. There was always a good natured competition between the two of us. Pierre had difficulty trapping in the wet environment, but he caught several beaver where he could get to the water. He wanted to set more mink traps, but he could not get around between the brush line and the deep water edges along the river.

Bob "Pierre" Hanson and myself with coyotes in front of the apartment we lived in.

We would skin every evening before going back to cook supper. We usually came in smelling like some sort of dead animal. I caught a couple little spotted skunks in bobcat traps, high up in some rocks. I wanted the hides to tan, since I had never seen one before. We were living in an apartment complex, and two young women living across the hallway, came over to complain about the odors that night when we came home. They were upset when they came to the door, and I am glad that old Pierre answered the door, because it wasn't very long, before he was laughing and joking with them, and invited them in for some cottontail supper. Like I said, he was smooth with women, and even though they were still grumbling about the skunk smell when they left, he had them laughing as well.

It seemed like we would catch one or two cottontail rabbits every day in our fox, coyote, or bobcat traps. We would clean them, and Pierre cooked some up one evening for supper. Dumb and naive as I was, I commented that I guess I was going to have to show him how to cook cottontail rabbits, since he had just fried them and they were quite tough. I did not know that Pierre considered himself quite a chef, and I could not have waved a red flag at a bull and gotten any more reaction than I got from Pierre with that comment.

So the next night I cooked up some cottontail rabbits, but I cheated, I cooked them in the crock pot, and used a can of cream of celery soup to cook them in. From that night on, it became a competition thing about every fourth day for one or the other of us, depending upon whose turn it was, to cook cottontail rabbits.

I am very glad that I spent that winter in Colorado with Pierre trapping. He was having trouble with his hip, on the side of his stiff leg. He would complain about that hip at night, after every day when we had done much walking. The following summer the hip bothered him bad enough to go to the doctor. It turned out that he had developed cancer and that it had progressed throughout his body. He died late that summer, in the hospital after they did surgery.

The next year, I trapped for almost a week in Northeastern Wyoming and a hard snow storm forced me to pull my traps. I then went to the sand hills in Nebraska, trapped for about another week, got very sick with some sort of food poisoning, and again pulled my traps and returned back home to Montana.

After Ed Courtney retired from the DEA, he moved to Boise, Idaho. He invited me to come and trap there, as he had purchased a nice large trailer home that we could park wherever we wanted to go trap. It took us almost two weeks to get everything set up and set a few bobcat traps out, when another deep hard wind driven snow storm forced us to make the decision to pull our traps. During that time Ed had been on the telephone with a mutual friend in California, and we headed to Southern California to trap.

I must admit that I was quite surprised at the animal numbers in California. I was a bit disappointed with the coyote numbers, as we were trapping in some low mountainous areas, but there were good numbers of small bobcats and gray fox. I was very surprised with the bear sign we saw and it seemed like there were mountain lions everywhere we went, as well as deer. Ground squirrels and small deer were everywhere, so food for any predator was more than abundant. I have no idea why there were not more coyotes in the area, as there were decent numbers of coyotes in the lower rolling hills closer to the coastline and in the agricultural areas.

It seemed like that winter Mother Nature kept playing tricks on us. Not quite dirty tricks, but just nasty enough to prove she was still in charge if she wanted to be. The deep snow, severe cold and hard winds in Idaho was a prelude to a small amount of snow in the desert of southern California and colder than normal temperatures for that area. We were behind locked gates, and had parked the trailer near an unoccupied dwelling, where we could hook up to the water, and use a three sided shed to skin and store fur. The light snow storm was heavy wet snow, and during the night a large oak tree split in half, from the weight of the wet snow, with half of it coming down, over the top of the shed, not quite touching the shed, and the big part of that half of the tree missing the pickup by just inches.

Maybe one of the worst mistakes I ever made in my life was when I got remarried the second time. My first marriage lasted for 25 years, the divorce was mutual consent, and I am still friends with her and her new husband to this day. The second marriage was not good from day one. I am not exactly sure why I got married, and have asked myself that question many times over and over. Details

Large oak tree limb that just barely missed hitting pickup.

are unimportant for this story, but what is important is that she was from England, and on one trip there I looked up a man by the name of Patrick Carey. Pat works there doing predator control work, as well as raising pheasants on a hunting preserve.

I spent a couple of days with Pat, checking his rabbit snares, and calling fox. Pat may just be the very best predator caller that I have ever met. He uses his mouth to call and squeaks on his fingers, producing a very realistic rabbit in distress sound.

The use of steel foothold traps is illegal in England, but I had managed to sneak a couple Lamb Saver traps and two Collar'um snare traps through airport security, since they had no idea what either was. The first day, we set them in a very populated area where a family was losing ducks near a pond in their front yard. The next day, I had two red fox, one in each of the Lamb Saver traps. So I can say that I did trap a bit in England and catch some red fox there. I left the traps there for Pat to use.

I also went fox calling with Pat and his wife (whose name is escaping me right now) one afternoon and one night. The daytime calling was fun, but not too much of anything very new to me, however the night time calling was unbelievable.

Pat would do the calling at night, carrying a shotgun to do the shooting, while his wife ran a very large, strong, battery operated light. When a fox's eyes were seen, his wife would put the light on very bright, while Pat, continuing to squeak and make cottontail rabbit distress sounds with his mouth and fingers, as he would just start to walk towards the fox. He would walk to within twenty yards of them and just shoot them, calling all the while. I was just dumb founded that it could be done, but I got to witness it happen five or six times that night. It was certainly an eye opening experience.

III - Slowing and Settling

O ver the years there are several wild animals that stand out in my memory. Two animals that consistently seem to pop into my memory are cottontail rabbits and skunks.

When I was quite young, I was hunting cottontail rabbits with my homemade long bow and arrows. It was all I could do to draw the bow back. In fact I could not pull it back if I held it properly, but if I laid it horizontally, I could pull it the length of the arrows I had made from willow sticks, with split turkey feathers, and crude broadheads constructed from a piece of copper pipe and a broken hacksaw blade. I killed several rabbits and even a few pheasants with those arrows. The bow supposedly pulled at around 60 pounds. I had big plans to someday kill a deer with that bow.

I was sneaking along under some rim rock cliffs, when I spotted a bobcat across the canyon. The bobcat was hunting too, and I was lucky to catch a glimpse of it as it made a short dash and crouched down.

As I watched the cat, my mind was spinning, of course wondering how I may be able to get a shot at the cat, but knowing I could never cross over the draw without being seen. I sat on a big rock and watched. The cat made two other short, quick, little dashes, and then pounced upon its intended victim. It caught a cottontail rabbit. I was amazed that it had been able to sneak that close to the rabbit. It then carried the rabbit to an open area, away from the low thick chokecherry bushes where it had caught the rabbit, and put the rabbit down. They both laid there for a few minutes, and the bobcat started poking the rabbit with its foot. When the rabbit started to run, the cat would jump on it, and then throw it in the air.

I watched him play cat and mouse games with the rabbit for a long time, before the cat tired of the game and began to eat the rabbit. The whole experience was very neat, and while perhaps nothing very unusual, it remains clear in my memory yet today, and I will admit that I have never witnessed a bobcat catch another prey animal.

I did witness two coyotes kill several lambs one very early morning. The coyotes had killed four lambs a couple days before, and I had walked into the area before daylight, hoping to get a shot at the coyotes. I was shivering, sitting with my back against some tall sagebrush, waiting for the sheep to get up from their bed ground. In the quiet cold windless morning, listening to a band of perhaps two hundred head of sheep awaken is an interesting experience in itself, as once they begin to awaken, the ewes bleat to the little lambs, and the little lambs begin to bleat back. The quietness is shattered by the continual noises.

Once the sheep were all on their feet, one of the old ewes started to walk quickly with some destination in mind, and the rest of the sheep instinctively began to follow, single file behind her. Suddenly the line separated apart, about one quarter of the distance behind the lead ewe. Then it separated again about the same distance behind where it had fractured the first time. One coyote was chasing a lamb where the sheep had separated the first time, and then a second coyote came through the line where they separated the second time, and it too was very close to catching a lamb that it was chasing. The noise of the sheep bleating and blatting became very frantic and loud, as all the sheep began to run in the direction they were going before the coyotes had surprised them.

Things were happening much too fast for me to get a shot, and I was having a difficult time seeing the coyotes with all the sheep running around them. Each coyote quickly caught the lamb they were pursuing, but then it appeared that each lamb managed to get away from the coyotes and began running toward the rest of the sheep. The coyotes started to chase after the escaping lambs, but ran past them, and grabbed another lamb from the escaping band of sheep, only to again have those lambs appear to escape the coyotes. I was having a difficult time believing that the lambs were strong enough to escape the coyotes, but it soon became apparent that in reality they had not, as the lambs began to stumble and fall, unable to gasp for air with their windpipes crushed and broken.

When the coyotes chased all the sheep over the top of the ridgeline, out of my view, I stood up and ran towards the top of that ridge. I almost ran into a fleeing lamb returning back over the top of the hill with a coyote not too far behind. I stopped when I saw the lamb, and when the coyote topped the hill and saw me, he stopped as well, long enough for me to get away a quick off hand shot. I hit the coyote too far back, and it ran, but it did not make it very far before it collapsed. When all the excitement was over, there were seven dead lambs and one dead coyote.

It was suddenly much easier for me to understand how and why coyotes would often kill several more lambs than just the one or two that they would eat a few bites of the tender parts from.

The only other time I ever watched a predator kill anything was when I saw three wolves before there was supposed to be any wolves in the area, chase five whitetail deer out onto the ice on the North Fork of the Flathead River. It was much different than the coyotes and sheep however, as the wolves would grab one of the deer as it slipped and fell on the ice, then begin to shake it like a rag doll. They killed all five deer, quickly, then wandered around on the ice edge, next to the flowing water, and returned the way they had came from, without eating a bite from the deer. Mother Nature has some cruel ways at times.

There must be a guardian angel somewhere whose job it is to look after fools, and he/she must need a rest after being assigned to me.

There is something about the early fall air, when the long hot summer finally begins to cool, that makes me want to sleep in the morning hours. I think it is just the enjoyment of drinking in the cool air and lavishing in the warmth of the blankets. Whatever it is, it did save my life one early morning.

I had seen several elk grazing in a hay meadow, at different times through out the summer. At times there would only be three or four elk in the meadow, while other times there were twenty or more. I would watch them go back into the timber, and then occasionally see them through the trees as they picked a travel route up a narrow salient ridge line leading to a plateau below much taller mountains.

The day before bow and arrow season was to open; I went

through the meadow, looking for somewhere that I might hide to get a shot at an elk. When I attempted to follow the route that I had saw the elk take, it soon became very apparent that the thick low brush and the steepness of the hill would be very difficult. I followed the elk trail as best I could up that narrow ridge, and found where the elk trail crossed over an old forest service trail. I followed that old forest service trail back towards where I left my vehicle. Even though the old trail had not been maintained in years, it was much easier traveling than attempting to climb that high narrow ridge. So I formulated a plan to be sitting where the elk trail and that old forest service trail crossed. I wanted to get there before daylight if at all possible, hoping to be in position before the elk started back up the side of the mountain to their day time resting area.

I slept in a bit later than I should have. I was disgusted with myself, so I left my vehicle and started walking as hard and fast as I could push myself. The sky began to lighten quickly, and I soon shut off my flashlight, and cursed myself for being so late. As I rounded a curve in the trail, it appeared that the trail had slipped away just ahead. Thinking that was a bit odd, since I had just walked down the trail the day before, I was straining to look ahead to pick a way through the rubble. As I came a bit closer, I could see below the trail where things had slid away to a pile of brush slightly covered with soil.

I am not too sure if I saw the elk leg sticking out of that pile of brush first, or the large head that was lying on top of the pile. I do remember well the taste of fear that filled my mouth. There is no other taste quite like the taste of fear. I had walked to within thirty or forty yards of a large Grizzly bear, laying on top of the elk that it had killed and attempted to cover by pulling down the side hill.

The bow and arrows in my hand suddenly felt like tooth picks. I came to a slow stop from the fast pace I had been walking. Then I attempted to take a slow step backwards. When I did, the bear moved slightly. I took another slow step, and the bear moved slightly again, and bared his teeth. I stood still for a short time before attempting another slow step backwards. The bear would not move, until I started to move. Each step I would make, the bear would slowly rise up a tiny bit. Then it started to mumble for a lack of better way to describe the real low sound that wasn't quite a growl. I then started talking to it in a low tone, as calmly as possible, telling him to just stay put, and that I wasn't interested in his stinking elk, and what a nice morning it was, and anything else that would pop into my head to say as calmly and soothingly as I could possibly sound, while slowly making steps backwards.

Then without warning, the bear suddenly, loudly popped his teeth! I about jumped out of my skin when it did. Without raising my voice, I did say, just a bit louder, "Whoa there big guy, I told you to just stay put, I don't want to fight and don't want you or your elk."

The bear was standing fully upright on all four feet as I was easing out of sight around the curve of the hill. He was still mumbling. When I got out of sight, I turned and began running as hard and fast as I could back down the side of that hill.

Had I not slept in that morning, I no doubt would have run right into that bear before daylight. As it was, I still consider myself to be very very lucky to have survived that morning, because a grizzly around food is not normally so tolerant.

I started to fish at a very early age. I have no idea how old I was, but I do remember catching my first trout on my step father's pole, and not knowing how to use the pole or reel, I just starting backing up, pulling the fish onto the shore, while my step father laughed and asked what the hell I was doing.

Every spring when fishing season opened up, the streams were always high and running hard, causing them to be muddy. The snow melt run off in the spring often made the larger streams very treacherous, as often there would be whole cottonwood trees floating and tumbling down the rivers. I would use worms for fish bait while the streams were still muddy, then as the winter snow run off would slowly trickle out, the streams would slowly clear and during that still high water period of time I would seine hellgrammites from the streams, and use them as bait. When full summer arrived and stream flows subsided to more normal levels, I would start to fish using grasshoppers for bait, or fly fishing with artificial flies that my grandmother and I would tie ourselves.

My uncle was an avid fly fisherman, as was my step father.

My uncle got into fly tying and bought a fly tying kit for my grandmother and me. We would tie flies and put them on a piece of cardboard to display them for sale at the local taverns and cafes. So I was always experimenting with some sort of new fly design. We used the feathers from the chickens that we raised. We raised Plymouth Rock chickens, primarily because of the feathers for tying flies, and we even sold many dried necks from the chickens to sporting good distributors, like Herter's Outdoor Supply Company.

A few days before I was to attend college, I loaded my fishing poles, to go to the Yellowstone River to attempt to fish for the ling that were suppose to be running at that time. I needed to stop and get some gasoline before I drove to the river. This was in the day of full service gasoline stations, and the individual that came out to pump my gasoline, spotted my fishing poles. We started a conversation about fishing that would eventually become a very strong friendship that lasts to this day.

Bill Bibeau is probably the most avid fisherman that I have ever known. He is a very good deer hunter a well, and loves to hunt, but he has a passion for fishing. Any kind of fish anywhere!

When paddle fishing first started in Montana, Bill and I use to take our growing families to the Missouri River, not too far from where Bill was raised, camp out on the banks of the Missouri River, and fish for paddlefish all day, and then run bait at night for catfish. For a couple of years, Bill held the state record for the largest caught paddle fish. I use to really seriously love the warm nights we spent on the banks of the river there, listening to birds sing and beaver flap their tails on the water in the river. We have fished in reservoirs, rivers, and of course large lakes.

Over the years, I have found myself fishing less and less each year. Oh, I still love to fish, but working, coyote trapping daily, I slowly began to realize that fishing was always just mostly an excuse for me to be out in nature. Since my work keeps me in nature, daily, I do not crave the contact like I use to in years gone by.

When I moved to Kalispell, Montana, I started fishing for bull trout, in the spring when they would run up the rivers. I would follow the run up the Flathead River, until the fish would eventually all trickle off into the small creeks. On a couple of these ventures, I

The Bill Bibeau that I know, usually with a beer in his hand.

stressed my guardian angel to the fullest.

My youngest half brother, myself, and my two best friends at the time were floating down the north fork of the Flathead River in rubber rafts, we came around a sharp corner in heavy current, and slammed into a log jam that went all the way across the river. We lost all our fishing equipment, and anything else that was loose in the rubber rafts, when all three rubber rafts were sucked under that large log jam. Everyone managed to go through under the log tangle without any injury. Rubber rafts were sucked under as well, but did not fare too well, and needed to be pumped on often as we proceeded to where our second vehicle was parked.

Because of that experience, that same summer I made a fiberglass canoe, because canoes are much more maneuverable in swift current.

However the following summer two of us were again floating down the north fork of the Flathead River; we rounded a corner, surprising a mother grizzly bear and two cubs. The strong flowing river was moving very fast, but we paddled the canoe as hard as we could towards the strongest rapids. We probably would have never made it past the upset mother bear, but when she let out her loud bawling growl, she started towards us, and then stopped to return to chase her cubs away from river edge to a tall tree that they began to climb. By the time she ran back to the river, we were past her, but she still jumped into the river to attempt to get to us, only we had a good lead and strong current. She went back to shore and ran back upstream towards her cubs.

Over the years, I have shot several black bears, but I have never had any wish to ever shoot a grizzly. Probably because something way down deep tells me that when they are gone, so will be much of what is so dear to me.

I have actually caught and held two bears in steel foot hold traps. One was a small cub. When I pulled up to the set, the mother bear and another young cub scurried away into the timber. I did not have a catch pole with me, so I attempted to push the cub in the trap down with my shovel so I could release it from the trap. It squealed and here came the mother bear out of the timber, woofing and growling. I jumped back into the pickup. She ran to the cub and swatted it with her front foot, evidently scolding it for not running after

Bear caught by only one toe in Carter County, Montana

her. She eventually wandered back towards the timber, and I got a snare out of the pickup bed. I put it on the cub, which immediately started to squeal again, and again here came Momma woofing and growling. I dropped the snare end, and again jumped back into the pickup. When the mother wandered slowly back towards the timber, I moved the pickup as close as I could to the cub, then picked up the end of the snare that was still around the cub, and pulled it towards the pickup. The Mother bear came back, but with the truck running she was reluctant to get too close, and I did finally manage to get the trap off the cub, who scrambled under the pickup. I had to be careful and slowly drive away.

The other bear that I caught was in Carter County, Montana. A very big surprise, as I had never seen any sign of a bear in all the years that I lived there, or never had heard anyone say anything about a bear. Surprisingly enough, I had people tell me of seeing moose, and even had people try to convince me that they had seen a wolverine, which I know is not true as the area is many miles out in rolling sagebrush lands, miles away from anywhere a wolverine

Beautiful spring bear trapped in Carter County, Montana.

could possibly have come from. So I am positive that if anyone had ever seen any signs of bear I would have heard about it.

I had seen mountain lion tracks on the four wheeler trail road two days before I set the trap that caught the bear, and for that reason I had used a #3 Bridger trap that had been modified with a base plate and four coil springs. I did not want a lion tearing apart one of my normal coyote traps. I have had several lions tear jaws out of coyote traps that are staked solid, so I did not want a repeat performance.

A sheep rancher that lived over the hill had lost a couple of lambs to coyotes, and the small dry creek bed where I set the trap had always been a good place to catch coyotes when they were in the area. It is inside the timber, but still on private property bordering the Long Pines Forest Service.

The Long Pines is a small forested area, just inside the Montana Border, next to South Dakota, and is actually an extension of the Black Hills Forest Service in South Dakota.

In order to get to the dry creek bed that I had to go up in order to reach the place where I had set the trap, I had to go through a long cattle pasture on both sides of the flowing Box Elder Creek, and drive across the creek on a rocky bottom area. The cattle in the area had seen my pickup many times, and rarely even looked up when I went through the pasture, but the day I caught the bear, they bellered and ran to the far corner of the pasture when they saw the pickup coming. I thought that was quite strange, but just assumed that perhaps the rancher had been working with the cattle, perhaps giving them shots, or other maintenance, before I arrived.

After I crossed through the water, I let my dog out to run ahead of the pickup. I did this regularly, as the dog would always find any fresh coyote signs that were in the area. There was a knoll that I had to drive over before I would be able to see the location where the trap was, and as we neared the area, the dog suddenly started to run hard and fast on the twin rut road trail ahead of me. I just assumed that I probably had a coyote in the trap, as the dog would often beat me to trap sites when he smelled a coyote before we could see anything, but when I topped the hill, he was barking at a black bear in the trap. Scared for the dog, I drove as close as I could, then ran to grab the dog, and get him away from the bear.

The bear did not seem too concerned that I was there, and was concentrating on the dog. I put the dog into the pickup, feeling lucky that he had not been swatted or killed. I grabbed my video camera and started to return to take some video of the bear, as when I had grabbed the dog, I saw that it was only caught by one toe.

Boy did I have to do some talking to myself, not to shoot the bear. It was a very beautiful bear. Not quite cinnamon colored, but a red brown color, with cinnamon colored long guard hairs. Since it was early spring, the bear had no rub marks on it, and must have just recently come out of hibernation. Since there were no bears in the area, I assumed that it may have been released in the area by the Fish and Game Department, even though I did not see a radio collar. So I left the area, and drove to the rancher that owned the land, to tell him about the bear, thinking it best to leave the decision up to him what to do about the bear. However, when I drove into the yard, all the neighbors where there, as they were branding calves, and it is common for all the neighbors to help with the chores on one ranch then go to the next ranch to help them brand. I am not too sure what the rancher may have wanted to do if he was there alone, but with all the other people around, we decided to release it.

We called the local veterinarian and the game warden. The vet used a tranquilizer gun to put the bear to sleep. It was full of large swollen wood ticks embedded in the neck behind his ears. By the time we finished, it was the healthiest bear around, as it got antibiotic shots, worm shots, and treated for the wood ticks.

Although the local game warden denied knowing anything about the bear being released in the area, it did come out later that they had released a few bears in that area. This same bear had to be trapped again later, by the Fish and Game in a culvert trap, and moved, as it got into trouble at a boy scouts camp.

Despite the many incidents with coyotes that are very memorable, I believe that the one that stands out the most in my memory is worth telling. I located some coyotes at daylight by blowing a siren that the coyotes howled back to. In the big open rolling sagebrush land of eastern Montana, I was able to spot the coyotes with my binoculars. By walking down the very bottom of a long dry creek bottom, I was able to keep the wind in my favor and get to where I thought was going to be one hundred yards away from the coyotes. It turned out to be only forty yards when I peaked over the top edge of the creek.

The coyotes had pups scattered in some large rocks that had fallen from a sandstone cliff. I saw several pups, but no adults. I lay on the ground, next to a large clump of sagebrush, watching and hoping to see an adult coyote to get a shot at. Most of the pups were just lying on, or near, the large sandstone rocks, sunning themselves in the early morning sun light.

As I lay there, the sun got higher, and warmer. A couple of deer flies started to bug me, and I was about to sneak back down into the creek bottom and leave when suddenly the pups all got excited and began boiling out of the rock pile. The female coyote came from some tall sagebrush to my left, and went to the pups.

The rubble of sandstone rocks had been part of the sandstone cliff at one time, and had just broken away. Some of the rocks were very large. One of the pup coyotes was on top of the larger rocks, and scrambling to get to his mother, he somehow slipped and fell over the edge of one of the large rocks. When he fell, he got caught in a V between two sharp angles of large rocks. He ended up hanging upside down with one hind leg wedged in the V crevice and his body hanging down. He began to squeal.

I had been concentrating too hard on watching the adult female coyote to see exactly how it happened that the pup became wedged in such a tight situation, but when he began to squeal, things really began to happen around the area. The female coyote ran towards the squealing pup, while all the other pups began to run back to the rock rubble to dive into holes and hide. The male coyote suddenly showed up and ran toward the squealing pup and his mother.

The larger male coyote bumped the female coyote, hard, with his shoulder, pushing her out of the way. He barked two or three gruff barks at the pup, and then turned to again block the female coyote from getting any closer. She howled, and the pup really began to squeal. The frustrated male coyote stood up on his hind legs and grabbed the squirming, squealing pup. He pulled hard, and when his efforts only pulled the pup tighter into the crevice of sharp corners, he braced his legs against the large rocks. The harder he pulled the louder the pup squealed at first, but then the large male coyote began to shake his head from side to side, violently. The pups squeals ended, but the male coyote braced himself again and shook his head harder. He pulled the pup away from the rocks, but he did so by pulling the body loose from the rear leg. He turned away from the rocks, walked a few feet, and then laid the lifeless body of the pup down. The female coyote rushed to the lifeless body and began to lick on it.

When the male coyote stopped walking, to turn and look back towards the female coyote and the lifeless body, I shot him. I sat up, and just sat there for a long time. I realized that I had just witnessed one of nature's harshest displays. Then I realized that I too had played a part in the final outcome of it all.

The large rolling sagebrush lands of Eastern Montana offer opportunities to see things from a long distance away. In the very early spring, when the snow is finally melting from the last remaining large snow drifts of winter; I have watched golden eagles kill migrating antelope and one young doe deer. Most of the kills I witnessed would be as expected, with the eagles hitting the fleeing animals and knocking them down. Rarely do they make the actual kill the first attempt, but after knocking the prey down the second or third time, they usually manage to complete the kill. However one kill I witnessed was totally different and something I would never have expected.

Two large golden eagles had singled away a doe antelope, and as it began to slow, one eagle dropped down and grabbed it with sharp talons in the middle of the antelope's back. Riding there, it spread its large wings, which caused the still running antelope to stumble and fall. As the antelope tumbled, the eagle hopped off, onto the ground, made a couple more hops and was again air borne. The antelope scrambled, regained its feet and began to run, but as it did the second eagle landed upon its back and spread its wings wide open, again causing the antelope to stumble and fall, only to one more time begin to run, but by that time the first eagle grabbed it again, holding on when the antelope fell. Then the second eagle that had become air borne by that time, landed upon the antelope as well. I was perhaps a full mile away on a long salient ridge top, but I could hear the poor antelope wail as the eagles began to feed from their fallen live victim.

When I contemplate about the experiences with various animals, two animals always seem to come to mind again: skunks and cottontail rabbits.

There was a large flat sandstone rock, it was only about twelve inches thick, perhaps ten feet long, but only four feet wide. It slid onto the steep side bank where a county road had been carved through a low rolling hill. The soft ground under the rock had eroded over time, and slid away from one end, making the rock protrude towards the roadway. I spotted a cottontail rabbit run and go under that end of the rock.

When I went to the rock, got down onto my hands and knees to peer under the protruding end, I could see the rabbit sitting looking at me. The rabbit was perhaps six feet away, just barely out of reach. I started digging away some of the soft soil, so I could slither under the rock, and attempt to grab the rabbit. When I reached for the rabbit, it lunged toward my hand. It made a huffing grunting sound, as it would lurch forwards, pouncing upon its feet. As my hand got closer when I strained hard, pushing against the rock bottom and the softer soil, the rabbit pounced upon my hand and bit the top of my middle finger.

Since I had raised many tame rabbits, and actually caught several wild rabbits using different methods, I was very surprised when the cottontail bit my hand. I had never been bitten by a rabbit, and never witnessed one become aggressive before.

After excavating some more loose soil, I finally managed to reach the rabbit and get a hold on it. It kicked, squirmed, and bit again, forcing me to drop it. Cussing the little rascal, I reached again, and this time managed to get a good solid hold on the rabbit, over its back. When I pulled it away, I saw why the rabbit had become so defensive. Immediately behind where the rabbit had been crouching, was a nest of hair, containing several new born, hairless, pink babies. Feeling very ashamed of myself, I released the rabbit back into the hole, and began to reconstruct some of the excavations I had created earlier.

I won't bore everyone and go into any details about any of the many hundreds of hours I have spent hunting for cottontail rabbits. Let me just say, that yet today, I enjoy a good meal prepared properly.

It is quite possible that I may hold the distinction of b e i n g the human squirted directly in the face by a skunk more times than any other human. Not exactly something to be proud of, for sure, but a distinction, none the less that few would care to compete against.

Every one of the stories would have to be about stupid mistakes that I made over the years. One time I was pulling a trap with a long chain from a hole, anticipating that it held a fox or raccoon, only to suddenly stare directly into the business end of a skunk, just in time to see the yellow liquid squirt directly into my face. Another time, while skinning a skunk, the scent gland broke, and splashed onto the side of my face. Another time, while cutting some very large thick cockleburs with a brush hook, I took a blind swing through some of the large flat leaves, towards what I thought would be the base of the bush, and in the process managed to cut the tail off of a skunk that had been hiding there. It sprayed as the flat leaves cleared a bit, and I was unable to escape, as I was entangled in the thick brush. However, I believe the worst time was while I was beaver trapping in the late spring.

During the winter while the snow was still deep, I located a beaver house with a large feed bed protruding through the ice in front of the hut. I walked on the hard frozen ice, up the long narrow winding creek that paralleled beside a larger river. I then chopped two holes through the ice and set a couple foot hold traps near the feed bed. Then a Chinook wind came during the night, warming the country quickly, and melting snow. When I returned to check my traps, I did not dare to attempt to walk up the ice, as water was running on top of the ice, and it was quite apparent that the ice was no longer solid enough to hold my weight. Knowing that the creek would rise quickly, I was worried about my traps being washed away, so I walked the narrow strip of land between the river and the creek.

As I neared the beaver hut, I had to fight my way through some thick willows, until I saw an area that contained no willows, and managed to push my way through to that open spot. It was a hump that stuck up higher than the surrounding landscape, immediately behind the beaver lodge. When I walked to the top of the hump, it suddenly all gave away, and an area approximately fifteen feet long and six feet wide, with me on top of it, fell about five feet, straight down.

There were two skunks curled up and asleep, lying on a slight ledge in the hole. At first they began to stir and slowly awaken. I moved slowly to the opposite side of the depression, and attempted to climb out of the hole. I got almost onto the top of the steep side when another large chunk of ground broke away. Falling, backwards, scrambling to hold onto the soil as it gave away; I somehow managed to smack the opposite side of the hole with my back, about a foot in front of the skunks. Since the dirt that I had been climbing was heavy when it fell onto me, my face was at the same level with both skunks when they sprayed. That was bad enough, but since my temper took over at that point, I grabbed my trapping hammer and dispatched both skunks with the hammer. I could no longer smell anything, and my eyes were still burning, so I am not too sure how much worse or how many more times I may have gotten sprayed through the ordeal. I know I had to get out of all my clothes in the cold back yard behind my house before the rest of the family would let me make a dash to the bathroom shower when I returned home.

The only spotted skunks that I ever trapped were in the low rolling mountains of northwestern Colorado. At first, believing they were just skunks, I attempted to treat them similar. It only took twice to realize they have better eye sight, and are much more nervous and quick to spray than other skunks are.

After the rubber padded traps had been introduced and used for a couple of years, the National Trappers Association needed some documentation to prove that regular steel foot hold traps were equally as humane. This was before the BMP (Best Management Practices) studies were thought about. They contacted me and asked if I would participate in the study by capturing red fox in the selected traps with an overseer for a couple of weeks. The idea was to use four different traps, one of them being a rubber padded trap, and records kept according to a protocol they had set up. Then the animal's feet were to be turned in for necropsy studies. I agreed to participate.

Mr. Bob Young was the state director from Georgia for the National Trappers Association and was the man assigned to be sure that I set the traps in proper rotation as well as handled the feet per trap correctly, so the trapper could not affect the results with his own prejudices per trap. Bob and I became friends during the time we spent on the study, and he invited me to come to Georgia and trap.

Had it not been for that study, I doubt very seriously that I would have ever considered coming to the southeastern part of the United States to trap. It is a long distance, something like twenty-four hundred miles, from Montana, and everything I had ever heard about the Deep Southeast was lots of people, swamps, alligators, snakes and bugs. Not that all of that is not somewhat true, but no area is quite what a person envisions by reading or hearing about it alone. I would have imagined that the fur would not be good on most animals, or certainly not good enough to attract me to come to such a strange area to trap. I knew nothing about the live market for predators, or nothing about what would be required to trap and market animals for the live markets. Obviously I learned a great deal during my first trip to Georgia to trap with Bob Young without actually realizing where it would eventually lead.

As I have been writing this story, it has came to my mind often just how lucky I am to have made the friends that I have made in my lifetime. Where would we be without our friends? Yes, family is important and leads us all in different directions, but I seriously believe our friends are often even more important than family for the roles they play and the influence they have to the directions our lives lead.

To start this segment, I suppose it would be only fair to describe Bob Young, and put him into the role, as a character, since that is the term I have used to describe many of the other friends who have influenced my life in some way or other.

Bob is a wiry tough "redneck," speaking with a very strong

southern accent, and is quite opinionated about many things. Perhaps a bit ornery in many ways, but with a tender side that he prefers not be seen. He is a recovered alcoholic, who makes no bones about it all. I have heard him say often that he did not drink beer very often, as he did not want a drink, he wanted to get drunk, so he drank only hard liquor.

Bob is very smart, very hard working, and talented in many different ways. His carpenter skills as well as metal working skill would rank with only the most talented in those professions, and most of what he knows has been self taught.

As with my other friends, there is a great deal more that I could write about to describe him, but believe that should be enough to start with to give you a general idea about his character.

Bob had built a few large holding pens from expanded metal to house the coyotes we would catch until we could find a buyer to purchase them. He also had done a lot of leg work to get written permission slips from landowners for us to trap their property. The pile of keys we had to get through gates had to be marked, as there were way too many to always remember.

Over the years, I've had several chances to visit with trappers from the eastern United States. I had also read a few trapping methods printed by eastern trappers. Every one of them claimed that LARGE dirt holes would not work in the East. My experiences with coyotes made me doubt those statements, to the point that I had gotten into several arguments, but of course I had no experience to prove my theories, so one campaign of my first trip there was to

Picture of the key ring that Bob Young and I had to carry daily to check traps in Georgia.

prove or disprove the large hole use with eastern coyotes. Whenever the ground was soft enough to use the tile spade to make a dirt hole, that is the size hole I made. Most of the coyotes that were caught while I was there were caught on LARGE dirt hole sets! I find it very interesting today to often read or hear some eastern trappers expound on the use of large dirt holes to catch coyotes and fox along the whole eastern tier of states.

I have also read and heard that it would be impossible to catch other animals where a possum had been caught in a trap. My own experiences with other animals have proven to me that predators are always interested where other animal odors are present, so I wanted to test the possum theories to the limit. To the point that I would often use smaller possums for bait down a hole with a trap in front of the hole. I caught coyotes, bobcats, and gray fox in the traps. So another theory out the window!

I will have to admit that I was totally surprised at the total number of coyotes where we were trapping. Having trapped coyotes all over the western United States, the thick brush, thorn vines tangled through the creek edges, and all the roads with people's homes close together, just seemed like unlikely coyote habitat. It still amazes me yet today how adaptable the coyote really is.

My first trapping trip in Georgia produced the first black coyote that I ever caught, although it did have a white spot on the throat.

I am going to get myself into trouble again here and say that I have never caught a black coyote that did not have dog in its genetic makeup someplace. Game departments want to deny this fact for some reason or other, however, white throats, white feet, white tips on tails, brown eyes instead of yellow, or yellow eyes with solid black fur, but larger skull and bones, has to come from somewhere. If it is not domestic dog, then I wish someone could explain a logical reason. Oh, guess I forgot! Wolf! While in Maine, I caught a red fox yellow colored large coyote, and biologists there want to say it is wolf DNA in the genetic make up. My question is which large domestic dog does not have some wolf DNA in the genetic makeup somewhere? Yet, show me yellow fox colored wolves, and prove to me that coyotes do not encounter more domestic dogs than they do

The first black coyote that I caught in Georgia.

wolves. I know Pedersen! You're just a trapper, not a biologist!

We also caught several otters on stock pond crossovers. It was the first time I had ever seen a pale brown otter. The otters in Montana are all a dark shiny black color, as too are many in Georgia, but the brown pale otters usually bring more money on the fur trade, since there are fewer of them.

Small bobcats and gray fox seemed to be almost everywhere and I will admit that I was surprised that several had very good quality fur. It would take a few more years and several more trips to Georgia, trapping, for me to realize that both seemed to always hang close to a reliable water source. That made a good deal of sense when trapping in the Desert Southwest, but seemed a bit illogical in Georgia, where annual rainfall amounts are usually over 70 inches per year, but even where streams are abundant and ponds are located regularly, the bobcats and gray fox seem to need to stay close to steady year round water sources. Probably because the bobcat and gray fox food sources depends on the water.

Videos were just starting to be sold for instructional trapping. It was Bob's idea that I make a video. I did not have a video camera, so he bought one and took pictures of our sets and the animals we caught while there on that first trip. Later after returning back home to Montana, I scrounged up enough money to buy a video camera and learned how to use it, taking pictures of my trap sets and animals caught in Montana to add to the video.

Then I ran into the problem of putting it all together; with no video editing experience or equipment to do so. More borrowed money spent for equipment; some useful, some just a total waste. This was before editing on a computer was feasible, as computers that could handle video cost almost ten thousand dollars apiece, since computer use, at that time, was also just starting to expand. Although I would not want to relive the frustrations of editing, pushing this button and that one at same time, with time lapses of equipment to catch up, while attempting to add sound at the same time, I believe I may be able to write a full book about that trying experience. If something malfunctioned, the entire editing process would have to be redone again, as everything was edited to one tape that would be the master tape for later reproduction. I have no idea how many hundreds of attempts I made, or how many hours were put into editing of the first video I put together. Let me just say that it was several weeks worth of work, working late into the night.

Technology was just starting to advance at a rapid pace, and the use of videos was popular. However, living in Montana, miles away from populated areas, finding a duplication house to reproduce the videos at a reasonable cost was difficult. Bob took over that part of the job, and traveled to Atlanta, Georgia to meet with a duplication house that could handle it. Since I was very short of money, Bob also financed that part of the entire operation.

When Bob Young ran into the difficulty of finding a place to purchase traps in Georgia, he decided to start his own business: Fox Hollow Trapping Supply Company. Having the equipment and knowledge to use it, he soon started laminating traps and adding base plates, so other trappers could purchase traps from him ready to be used on the trap lines for the live market. One thing led to another, and I gave him some lure formulas to use, so he could make his own line of trapping lures. With his own property to use as a base, and the wood working tools and skills to build with, and the metal tools and skills, combined with a hard working determination to succeed, he built a quite successful business.

Since it was his idea originally, and with money invested in the video operation, his business became the distribution center for all the videos that I made. We split the profits equally.

For several years, I would start fur trapping in Montana, and then come to Georgia to trap during December, January, and February.

During the winter of '05-'06 I trapped in Montana, and then went to Iowa and Missouri to trap with plans of again coming to Georgia to trap. However, the man who had given me a cabin to stay in while I was in Missouri had a serious beaver problem, and I remained there attempting to catch the last few beaver from his creeks and ponds longer than I should have, so I did not make it to Georgia that winter to trap.

So I returned to my home in Montana for only two days. I shoveled my way through several snow drifts, and drove through a pasture to get to my house because of all the deep snow there. I did not have all my equipment unloaded yet from the pickup, when I received a phone call from Georgia. The man wanted to offer me a full time year around job with a home to live, but I would need to be in Georgia within three days for an interview. It takes three days of hard driving to get that far in the winter!

To make a very long story short, I made that three day trip, then went back to Montana and gave the woolgrowers organization the necessary sixty day notice that I would be quitting the job in Carter County, and moving to Georgia.

The sheep industry had been suffering for quite awhile at that point. The main reason is because the leaders of the national organizations refuses to make any changes while the rest of the world is progressing. The sheep industry has been selling 80 to 100 pound lambs for two hundred years, and shearing sheep by hard physical hand labor, while cattle, hogs, and farming industries have been steadily producing larger and larger animals and mechanizing agricultural machinery to cut back on actual physical labors. I could see a steady decline in younger people remaining in the sheep business as the older generation was melting away, and could see the hand writing on the wall for the future of my work, doing predator control work, with the sheep industry. Especially since the government could, and would love to price me out of the picture easily, at any time.

I felt very fortunate to have the opportunity arise to do predator control work in Georgia. At this time, I certainly have never regretted having made the change and move. Amazing how things seem to work out sometimes if a person just keeps working hard and improving.

Southern hospitality is an expression that stretches way back, and is still a way of life today in the South. Yes, there are some rude people, yet, while I am going to find this very hard to describe, they have an off handed way of being impolite that is almost respectful. "Yes Sir, No Sir," and "Yes Ma'am, No Ma'am," are used to answer almost any direct question, before any explanation that may follow. Treating others with some form or other of respect really is a way of life in the South.

Southern accents vary dramatically from area, to area, with often times very short distances between the changes. Black people seem to have their own accent, and even they seem to change a few short miles away. It came as no surprise to me that I would not always understand everything that was being said, but since everyone watches television and listens to the radio, it surprises me constantly that people often have a difficult time understanding me when I talk. Guess I have more Montana drawl than I realized. I suppose that I have had to learn this several times, in other states before as well, wherever I notice a dramatic accent. Minnesota to Maine to Iowa, New Jersey, to Texas all are different, while everyone speaks the same English language, yet the Deep South seems to have the most variation in accents in very short distances. Although the very brief amount of time I spent in England, I learned quickly there, that a few short miles will put total different accents and slang terminology into the language, more than any other place that I have ever been.

As anywhere, a person has to prove themselves with honesty and returned respect, before local people welcome you into their community. I spent a good deal of effort and time to try to understand what southern people expect. Then I have had to prove to most of the landowners in the area that I really am just a trapper and not using that as an excuse to gain access to their property so I could hunt deer, turkeys, hogs, quail, or go fishing in the many ponds. Word of mouth is still the best advertising there is, and slowly the people have started asking me to trap on their property, since no one seems to like coyotes, and once people started seeing coyotes regularly in my truck or in traps, more people contact me now; which is great, since I hate pounding on doors to meet people for the first time and asking for permission to trap.

Perhaps most of the adjustment I have had to make is learning how to deal with very regular, hard, down pouring rains, and keeping traps working throughout those times. From late spring until early winter, learning to live with high humidity as well as days of intense heat along with the humidity, is one adjustment I may never get use to, but when I make that statement to the local people, most will quickly reply that they were born and lived here most of their life and that they too will never get adjusted to it. It is something that has to be experienced to totally understand.

Learning how to live with all the biting insects is another problem, as are the many different kinds of snakes that come out when it is warm. I guess while I am on this subject, I am always amazed that there are not more mosquitoes than there are. I believe even cold Montana has more mosquitoes than there are here in the swamp covered lands of southern Georgia. However what they lack in mosquito population, they make up for quickly with fire ants, more different kinds of deer flies than I have seen anywhere else, and although they do not bite, the cussed small gnats that are literally everywhere when it is warm attempting to get into your eyes, ears, nose, and mouth.

A day rarely goes by that I am not amazed that coyotes have learned to adapt to live in this region. Anywhere that there is not heavy thick brush, vines with thorns, and briars in the low wet areas, there are people moving almost always somewhere close by. I guess that I understand that they learn how to figure out the schedules of people, and adjust around that, since they are now found living in almost every major city in the USA, however I have been learning, slowly, that they have had to change many of what I would normally call instinctual habits, as well. By way of a couple quick examples: The coyotes here do not travel very large areas, and they do not fill in where coyote voids are formed very quickly. Coyotes here seem to be more vocal year around, than anywhere else that I have spent any time. I have learned that you can actually trap all the coyotes out of an area here and it may take as much as three years before other coyotes move into the locality. (All of which has made my job here quite easy once the initial coyotes are caught.) My personal theory on the vocalization, is that they need to become quite vocal while hunting the thick brush edges, to both move prey that live in the thick stuff, as well as to keep track of where each coyote is hunting. Why they do not fill in vacant areas as quickly as they seem to do everywhere else I have ever been still remains a bit of a mystery to me, but my theory at this time, is that they do not travel as far or as regular here because of all the roads and people in the area.

Traveling in less populated country throughout the USA, I find that as soon as I believe I know something about ground soil and moisture, be it rain or snow, freezing, or thawing temperatures, or even nice dry warm conditions, the less I can relate what I learn in one locality to a totally different terrain. That revelation, could possibly explain one reason I manage to get my vehicle stuck as often as I do.

Going way back to when I was learning to drive in Montana, the first hard lesson I needed to learn was that snow drifts, get hard enough to easily support a vehicle, then I learned about mud that a human could easily walk upon, would sink the tires of a vehicle. Then I learned that rocky soil in the mountains would get muddy enough to get a vehicle stuck if the vegetation found enough soil to grow thick in. It was not too long before I needed to learn about heavy clay soil, or often referred to as pure gumbo in the rolling prairie lands of Montana. The gumbo gets almost rock hard when dry, then with a light rain it will become slicker than grease on the surface, but almost bottomless anywhere water would accumulate for any length of time. All this is perhaps quite basic, yet believing I had learned, the hard way, I was soon to learn while traveling out of state, that similar looking soils, may, or probably not, produce quite similar results. Soil texture, coloration, and ability to support vegetation mean nothing actually.

In the rolling prairie lands of eastern Montana, the soft clay soils sometimes quickly turn into bentonite laden soil with little coloration variation, and driving a vehicle in one is nothing like driving in the other. I had at times been able to cross the landscape by staying off of the bentonite soil vehicle trails, and driving cross country through grass and sagebrush for awhile, but the mud picks up on the tires, mixing with bits of vegetation, until it eventually will pack so tight in the wheel wells that a vehicle does not have enough power to make the tires even spin, much less be able to turn the front wheels well enough to steer a vehicle. I have used broken steel fence posts to chop and dig the mud out between the tires and wheel wells, and gone another fifty yards and had to dig more of the mess out again.

Most local landowners were born and lived their whole life on their holdings. Each has learned how a vehicle will get around and the results of vehicles traveling the land. In Montana, when the snow drifts would accumulate on normal traveled roadways, it was common practice to get off the road when possible to drive around the snow drifts, but in Colorado, Iowa, or Missouri, it was totally taboo to drive off the roads. Most farmers expect you to stay on established four wheel trails while driving through their fields, yet here in the southern Georgia, you are expected to drive around the fields, tight to the edges, which would probably get you in deep trouble in most of the rest of the farm country in the USA.

Very sandy soils are totally different again. The sand will pack tight where vehicles travel regularly, and water may stand in the vehicle tire ruts, but it will remain firm enough to drive on easily. Most other soil conditions will become deep mud where water stands very long, but in the sand country, just the opposite is true. When it gets real wet, it is wise to remain in tire tracks in the sand, as driving just outside of the tire tracks may sink you very deeply in slick wet sands. Being stuck in the sand is much like being stuck in other mud conditions except even when a vehicle is jacked up, so something can be put under the wheels, the loose sand will fill the tire hole quicker than a person can place rocks or other more firm debris that may support the vehicle under the tires. When the vehicle is lowered, the sand that slid into the depression will be softer than what was there initially. In eastern Montana, I often carried tire chains. The chains saved me often enough in deep snow conditions or light mud. For deeper mud, I carried four, five foot long boards to place under the tires. In the sand country, tire chains will get you in trouble quickly, and four boards under the tires will just slide out from under the tires on the loose sand with the vehicle not even moving. I have had to learn that a piece of canvas tarp is much better than a board for the sand. Here in the wet swamp sand country I now carry four eight foot long by three feet wide heavy pieces of canvas to put under tires on the sand.

With the different soil types, things get even more complicated while setting traps in different moisture and levels of heat. George Good showed me about using coal shale in Montana, as the fine dusted coal tended to repel moisture and allowed a trap to come through it easily while closing. Gumbo becomes very sticky and heavy when it absorbs any moisture it comes into contact with, and traps stick to the soil wanting to pick up globs of the heavy soil as they go closed. Normal black top soils will vary drastically as some seem to repel moisture a bit, while others absorb it like a sponge, and yet others will almost act like heavy sticky bentonite gumbo soils. While trapping in any new area it takes time, not to mention the frustration at times, to experiment a bit with the different soils available in the area to learn which works best.

Every new area a person traps in will also take time to learn about the animals in the area. Often, a trapper will find that trapping pressure has been heavy before he arrived and animals become a bit educated, and learning what they know will take time and a bit of frustration again. Also problem animals such as pesky fingered raccoons that love to dig up traps, or a heavy population of skunks, or possums that will insist on messing up good predator sets will need to be learned about. Here in Georgia, there is also the cussed armadillos that will spring traps often with their stubby short legs and hard exterior shell which the trap jaws hit first pushing the animal upwards quicker than the jaws can close on their short legs. Of course each area will harbor different kinds of predators and different populations of predators.

I have learned that coyotes will vary in size in many different places. Bobcats will vary a good deal in size, while red and gray fox tend to vary little in actual size, even though there are a few places where they do tend to be a bit smaller than most other places.

It stands to reason that most predators inhabit very similar type habitats throughout the USA; yet, everything will adapt and change their habits to fit what is available where they live. Mother Nature has some marvelous ways of adjusting.

The poor red fox are almost always chased and killed by coyotes. In normal red fox habitat, of wide open grasslands or fields, the larger coyotes easily chase the red fox and catch them. As coyotes keep increasing and expanding their living areas, fewer red fox survive, and most that do, move close to where people live, often into the edge of city limits, or perhaps den up in the barrow ditch of busy roads. Here in the Southeast, I am amazed to slowly learn that many red fox have adapted and now live in the thickest swamps, or wet creek bottoms, where they often share the same habitat with gray fox.

IV - Feeling My Age

For the last couple of years, I find that I am starting to feel my age. Now and then I will awaken and find that some part of my body will ache, to remind me of an old injury that I had all but forgotten about. The knee injury that I told the story about seems to rarely bother me, after I had part of the meniscus removed that was floating around and becoming lodged in the joint. It has never locked up again, but will feel weak after a very long hike. The fingers that were caught in the Conibear trap only ache when it is cold. So I suppose I could say that my outdoor experiences are not the source of most of my aches and pains.

Stupidity on the other hand is a different story! A bar room fracas that caused me to hit my hip on the sharp corner of the foot step railing while tussling took a long time to heal, and causes me a good deal of misery if I over do things today.

While working alone in a full service gasoline station while in college, I was attempting to change the antifreeze in a young man's car. I also had to run outside and pump gasoline every time a customer pulled up to the pumps. The kid was working on his radio, installing a reverberator or something.

I came back inside after pumping gasoline, and reached down to tighten the petcock on the radiator. I had my arm beside the fan, and was balancing myself by holding onto the fan belt that went to the alternator with my other hand. I heard the click of the solenoid on the starter. Fearing for my arm next to the fan, I was attempting to remove that arm as quickly as possible when the motor caught. I managed to clear my arm from the fan, however the hand holding the belt was whisked into the pulley of the generator. It broke the fan belt, but not before it broke all four of my fingers.

Pain makes my temper react. I came around the side of the car to where the kid was sitting, with the intention of hurting something! The look of fear on the kid's face stopped me, momentarily, but still angry, and going to hurt something, I grabbed one crooked finger and straightened it, then another, and yet again one more, but the exertion and pain of that suddenly made me feel very weak and a bit sick. I was not capable of straightening the last finger at that point, so went to the hospital emergency room to have the last finger set, and the hand put into a cast. Those fingers will often ache today.

I do not have the endurance or strength that I use to have, and find that very frustrating at times, and for the last week or so, I have been treating my right side very gingerly after pulling a muscle while lifting a large container of water to water coyotes in a holding pen.

There are days, when it is raining, or when it is very cold, or extremely hot, especially when accompanied by high humidity, that I now find myself lacking a bit of motivation to get started. Still I find that I crave contact regularly with nature in some form or another. Normally all it takes to get me started and get over the lack of motivation is to open the door and step outside.

Joints will often stiffen while muscle aches do not rub out so easily when over stressed a bit, like they use to do.

The man that I now work for has two places, one on the east side of Georgia, and one on the west side of the state. I live and do most of my predator control work on the place at the west side of the state, and there are two other trappers that work the place on the east side of the state, however when they run into problem animals that they are unable to catch, I have to go there to deal with the problem animals. I just returned home after having to trap for two weeks on the other place. While I was there, I caught a very large old beaver that moved into a pond next to the home place and was chewing down trees in the yard, as well as a large old coyote that was following the truck around putting out pen raised quail. I found myself feeling a particular closeness with both of those large old animals.

The coyote had seen just about every imaginable set, and avoided most of the best lures available on the market today. He stepped into one of my traps situated where I had dug a trench back into vegetation along the edge of a mowed area to plant a new growth of feed for the birds that are being raised there. The shallow trench was dug back into vegetation about four feet, and an old bleached bone with lure had been situated at the far back edge of the trench. The trap had been set at the edge of the mowed vegetation and the trench, and blended in as much as possible. A stall out area, I would term it, where an animal would stop to look at the lured bone, without having to get close, or step onto any loose soil in the trench.

When I walked up to the old coyote, his age was showing, and he turned to square away with me, rather than attempt to struggle hard and get away. The look on his face and in his eyes told me that he knew he had messed up good, and probably for the last time in his life. I found it difficult, because for some reason or other I felt like I shared a bit of his emotions and understanding.

I believe I have stated many times, how blessed I have been to be able to live the life that I have. Living in close contact with nature, experiencing the best and some of the worst has been a wonderful life.

There are still a few places I would like to see and experience, as well as a very few animals that I would like to learn about and trap for. Wolverine and fisher are two that come to mind quickly. Yet, even that calling seems much weaker than it used to be.

I suppose that time is reminding me that I will not be able to go everywhere and experience everything nature offers, because my body will not hold out that long. Plus my guardian angel is probably looking forward to an easier assignment as well. But I will attempt to remain in contact with nature as long as possible.